UNITED STATES POLICY
and THE THIRD WORLD

Problems
and
Analysis

UNITED STATES POLICY
and THE THIRD WORLD

Problems
and
Analysis

CHARLES WOLF, JR.

LITTLE, BROWN AND COMPANY
BOSTON AND TORONTO

To my Parents

Foreword

The term "third world" (*tiers monde*) is a Gallic phrase that is both artfully ambiguous and occasionally useful. The two other worlds implied by the term are the economically advanced democracies, and the communist countries. Thus, the third world is usually considered to embrace all the underdeveloped noncommunist countries, and will be so considered in this book.

One of the ambiguities in the three-world classification is that it appears to leave some countries (for example, Spain, Portugal, South Africa) out of the world. Another ambiguity arises from the fact that this classification may conceal divisions that exist within each group and which, for some purposes and issues, are more significant than the divisions between groups; for example, the Sino-Soviet rift, and the fissures within the Western alliance. Furthermore, the threefold partition of the world implies that there is more homogeneity *among* countries of the third world than between them and countries of the other two—an implication that is highly debatable. The Philippines, India, and Brazil, for example, have considerably more in common with the economically advanced democracies than they have with most African countries.

Nevertheless, as part of the title of this book, the "third world" has some advantages over the terms with which it is often used more or less synonymously. Some of these synonyms have an invidious connotation ("*under*developed" or "*less*-developed"), and some of them are inaccurate or positively misleading (most of the "developing" countries are not yet, in any real sense, developing at all). But there is another reason why "third world" is more appropriate in this book's title. The terms that carry some form of the word "development" have by now acquired an economic and technological flavor. Because they have been most frequently used in the context of *economic* development, they convey a suggestion that the problems and policy issues that arise in these countries are mainly due to a *lack* of economic development; hence, economic development appears to be the main remedy. "Third world," perhaps because of its ambiguity, has come to imply—more accurately, in my view—that the problems of these countries are imbedded in an international and domestic context in which political, social, and military, as well as economic, considerations are powerful. This wider context is more appropriate to the subject matter of this book, although some of the discussion is concerned with issues of *economic* development more narrowly construed.

One other point about the title. Although the focus of the book is on the third world, the viewpoint reflected in most of the discussion is that of the United States in its relations with these countries. Most of the discussion is concerned with formulating and understanding third-world problems in order to consider how improvements can be made in the policies and programs with which the United States pursues its aims, aims that often coincide with but sometimes diverge from those of the highly heterogeneous countries of the third world.

This book has been written since the publication of my book, *Foreign Aid: Theory and Practice in Southern Asia*, in 1960. The individual chapters share with that study a concern with problems of United States policy toward the third world, and in particular a concern for the analytical underpinnings and implicit assumptions behind policies and programs.

The chapters themselves have several methodological and substantive themes in common. Methodologically, they seek to clarify terms and to test relationships that are often taken for granted. For example, the question of the "importance" or "value" of the less-developed countries to the United States, and assertions about "self-help" as a condition of United States aid to these countries, arise frequently in both public and academic discussions without clarification of what the key terms mean, or of how their meaning relates to United States policy. Similarly, assumptions and assertions are often made about the political effects of military aid programs, or of economic development programs, without any attempt to formulate the assumptions so that they might be tested against such evidence as is available. In another context, much academic as well as policy discussion of insurgency or "liberation wars" in the underdeveloped world is based on an implicit theory of how such movements get started and flourish, with little attention devoted to making the theory explicit, so it can be carefully examined, or to considering alternative theories.

The chapters in this book try to deal with these questions by fairly precise reasoning from explicit premises. Several chapters try to extend this reasoning by testing the resulting hypotheses against some of the relevant empirical data, occasionally using statistical techniques or other methods to provide tests for the hypotheses.

Substantively, the chapters are concerned with both the conflicting and the complementary relationships among political, military, and economic conditions in the less-developed countries, and among United States policy instruments that are intended to affect these conditions. Many of the chapters are, like my earlier study of foreign aid, directly concerned with how the use of economic and military aid, as major instruments of United States policy in the developing countries, can be made more effective: by setting up clearer criteria for allocating aid funds, by taking advantage of potential complementarities between military and economic programs, and by seeking to minimize potential or actual conflicts between these programs. Many of the problems discussed in the book apply broadly to the third world, but some of the chapters and some of the data deal with particular countries such as Vietnam and Korea, or with particular regions such as Latin America and Southeast Asia.

The book is divided into two principal parts, differing in style and content. Part One considers several general factors that affect United States policies toward the third world. It is concerned broadly with connections among political, military, and economic problems, and with their bearing on United States policies. Chapter One, "The Value of the Third World," considers the broad question of the "value" of the less-developed countries to the United States in terms of the separate but related military, economic, and political components of United States interests in these area. How much are Laos, Vietnam, or Cuba "worth" to the United States, and what is a useful way to think about this question? In the light of this discussion, Chapter Two, "Connections Between Political, Economic, and Military Problems," considers the broad relationships among political, economic, and military factors in the developing countries, and the problems which these relationships pose for United States policies and programs. In particular, Chapter Two explores the relationships among economic growth, redistribution of wealth and opportunity, and the role of force, in the modernization of the less-developed countries. With these broad relationships as background, Chapter Three then takes up the specific problem of insurgency in the third world, and advances an alternative to the analytical framework with which these problems are usually approached. At the opposite end of the spectrum of violence, Chapter Four considers the uses and limitations of nuclear deterrence in preventing or meeting conflicts that arise in the third world.

By contrast with Part One, which is general and theoretical, Part Two is empirical and quantitative. The chapters of Part Two are more technical and varied, and most of them grew out of RAND research conducted over the past several years. Chapters Five and Six, focusing on Latin America, examine the political effects of military and of economic programs. Both chapters try to give empirical content to some of the broad relationships discussed in Chapter Two. The two chapters use similar methods and Latin American data to test several hypotheses concerning the political effects of military programs and of economic programs. Chapter Seven, "Defense and Development," considers the relationship between defense and development in several countries, and specifically examines how it may be possible to realize approximately equivalent military effectiveness from military programs while achieving substantially enhanced economic side effects. Chapter Eight turns to economic development and economic aid programs, and in particular to the question of how the development performance of less-developed countries might be assessed objectively. One operational aim of this discussion is to give some workable meaning to the requirement stated in United States foreign aid legislation that aid allocations be partly based on the extent to which recipient countries are engaging in effective measures of self-help. Chapter Nine then considers ways in which the effectiveness of United States aid programs can be improved by specific methods that provide for better coordination between economic and military programs.

Finally, Chapter Ten, "Research and Policy," presents some concluding comments on the uses and limitations of research, drawing examples from the preceding discussion.

Although the chapters are concerned with policy problems, only in a few cases do the analyses lead to policy conclusions. In these cases, the results (relating, for example, to the coordination of military and economic aid, to the measurement of self-help, to the design of counterinsurgency programs, and to the political effects of military programs) may have had some influence on United States policy and procedures, although it is hard to be sure in these matters. On the other hand, several chapters are inconclusive with respect to policy conclusions, and are concerned instead with questioning accepted views and suggesting new lines of inquiry, rather than with reaching firm conclusions.

Most of the chapters have resulted from RAND research studies, and several have previously appeared as RAND research memoranda. I am indebted to The RAND Corporation for making this material available and thereby facilitating publication of the book. In these studies I have had the benefit of comments and assistance from present and former colleagues, including Luigi Einaudi, Herbert Goldhamer, Richard Kao, Nathan Leites, Richard Moorsteen, Anthony Pascal, George Rosen, James Schlesinger, Roberta Wohlstetter, and Albert Wohlstetter. Janina Bonczek and Hiroshi Noguni provided valuable research and computing assistance for several of the studies. I also wish to express my appreciation to the editors of *Economic Development and Cultural Change, Operations Research, World Politics, ORBIS,* and *The Yale Review,* and to the Institute of Strategic Studies, for some of the material in this volume which they have previously published. Finally, it is a pleasure to acknowledge the meticulous editorial assistance I have received from David Giele of Little, Brown and Company.

Contents

xiii

List of Tables

UNITED STATES POLICY
and THE THIRD WORLD

Problems
and
Analysis

Part
One

GENERAL CONSIDERATIONS
AFFECTING POLICIES
AND PROGRAMS

The Value of the Third World

What is the importance or worth of the third world to the United
States? What is the value to the United States of changes in the
status and orientation of these countries? Should we be concerned
about the less-developed countries for any reasons other than a sense
of humanity and a general preference for the well-being and advancement of peoples everywhere?

Put this way, the question seems crass. But it is a question that
inevitably arises whenever one considers a possible commitment
of United States resources in these countries—whether in the form
of economic or military aid, or of United States military forces, or of
diplomatic undertakings and guarantees. The question arises most
acutely when one considers the international trouble spots that have
involved major United States policy issues and commitments in recent years: Cuba, Laos, Taiwan, and Vietnam, to take several examples.

Although the question is not answerable in any precise sense, some
useful things can be said in approaching it and in trying to distinguish
between more and less unsatisfactory answers to it. This chapter will
be mainly concerned with describing and illustrating a method that
may help to clarify and facilitate meaningful discussion of the
question.

In principle, of course, a discussion of the value of "other" countries to the United States includes some consideration of the advanced countries, most significantly of Western Europe. However, this book will be primarily concerned with the value of the less-developed countries, and more particularly with their value in certain extreme contingencies to the United States in this generation. To illustrate the general approach, examples and data will be mainly drawn from Southeast Asia.

"Value," of course, cannot be measured with a single yardstick. At the outset, it is worthwhile to distinguish between values, or components of value, that can be *quantified*, and those components that can be expressed only in *qualitative* terms.

The components of value that can be quantified are those to which the concept of *alternative cost* is applicable: When a specified outcome can be achieved in more than one way, the maximum value of any particular way is the *lowest* cost among the alternatives. For some aspects of value, the notion of alternative cost can be usefully applied to obtain a rough numerical estimate. For both the military and the economic components of value, this approach has merit and applicability.

However, for other components of value this approach does not make sense. When we discuss the political, psychological, and ideological components of a country's value to the United States, the alternative-cost approach does not help. It would, for example, be generally accepted that for political and ideological reasons the United States favors the emergence of freer, more democratic and open societies in the less-developed areas. We prefer a world in which these characteristics are more prevalent to one in which they are less prevalent. Hence, we are, and should be, willing to devote effort and resources to help countries to move in this direction. But it is not clear how much the political and ideological components of value are worth, nor is it likely that we can think meaningfully about them in quantitative terms. For these aspects of value, we simply have to rely on opinions, discussion, and judgments. Moreover, these qualitative aspects of value may well dominate the ones that can be quantified. This does not mean, however, that we should refrain from trying to identify the relevant numbers wherever we can. Nor does it mean that all ways of expressing the qualitative components of a country's value to the United States are equally clear, comprehensive, and useful. One can be qualitative in better and worse ways, just as one can be quantitative in better and worse ways.

QUANTITATIVE COMPONENTS OF VALUE

Fortunately, some aspects of the value of other countries can be approached quantitatively. Here we shall suggest a method that might be employed in measuring these values, as well as a rough indication of some of the numbers that might result. The adjectives "large" or "substantial" will be used to suggest five-year costs that are conjectured at, say, over a billion dollars, whereas "small" will mean that the cost is below this threshold.

MILITARY VALUE

The maximum military value of a country can be estimated by assuming the country's "loss," formulating several different military scenarios, and then asking what costs the United States would have to incur to offset the loss of the country if these military contingencies actually arose. In this context the term "loss" is used in a complete and unsophisticated sense to mean simply that the country becomes communist, and that the Soviet Union or China or another communist country is enabled to derive whatever military benefits the area might confer on them. This purposely extreme assumption does not imply that such a loss is the *only*, or even the *most likely*, alternative to an existing relationship between the United States and the particular country; the assumption is made simply to provide an upper bound to that country's military value to the United States.

Note that this approach construes "loss" in terms of a one-way change. The chance that a country might be able to reverse its status within the relevant time period is ignored.[1] In this context, "the relevant time period" is one in which the broad pattern of recent inter-

[1] The assumption of irreversibility could be dropped from the following discussion if there were some way of estimating the probability of reversal within the relevant time period. For other references to the irreversibility assumption, see Chapter Two below, pp. 25, 35.

national relationships is assumed to exist. Communist attempts to expand influence and control are assumed, whether by the Soviet Union, China, or another communist country, acting alone or in concert; and resistance to such expansion is assumed on the part of the United States. No distinction is made between the value of a country at different points in this time period, although such a distinction could be made within the framework of this discussion.

This notion of value can be illustrated more concretely. Consider a scenario in which there is a buildup by North Vietnam, China, or the Soviet Union of a substantial capability within South Vietnam and Thailand for waging guerrilla war against the present governments in those countries. Now, assume the loss of Laos. The military value of Laos can now be estimated by examining several different kinds of costs that would have to be incurred in order to maintain a *counter*-guerrilla capability in Vietnam and Thailand sufficient to offset the assumed loss of Laos. One cost would lie in providing enough additional surveillance along the 700-mile border between Laos and Thailand, and the 200-mile border between Laos and South Vietnam, so that the support or buildup of guerrilla manpower would be as difficult (that is, as costly) to the communists as it would have been had Laos not changed status.

Now assume that despite this surveillance some increase occurred in the flow of guerrilla manpower and supplies into Thailand and South Vietnam. As a supplement to the surveillance costs, Thai and Vietnamese paramilitary forces would have to be increased to limit guerrilla incidents to some "acceptable" level.

Another example might involve a direct invasion of Thailand or of South Vietnam by a Viet Cong, or combined Chinese and Viet Cong, force of consequential size. Here, the value of Laos might be estimated by calculating the increase in Thai and Vietnamese forces that would be required to defend as effectively against an invasion starting from the Laotian borders with South Vietnam or Thailand as smaller forces would defend against an attack that began several hundred miles farther north from North Vietnam's borders with Laos. With longer supply lines for the attacking force, and increased warning time for the defense, an invasion that must first cut through Laos would be at a clear disadvantage. The larger defending force needed for equivalent effectiveness is a measure of this disadvantage, and hence of the military value of Laos in this contingency. In other words, the costs of defending Thailand and South Vietnam tend to rise substantially if Laos is lost. The amount of that increase reflects the military value of Laos.

Note that in both these scenarios the value of Laos is related to contingencies involving countries other than Laos itself. This is one of the ways in which the "house-of-cards," or "dominoes," analogy, which has sometimes been applied to the countries of Southeast Asia, is valid. A loss of Laos (or of South Vietnam) increases the vulnerability of neighboring countries. Stated another way, such a loss requires that additional costs be incurred if the vulnerability of neighboring countries is not to increase.[2] This is not to say that the dominoes fall automatically or inevitably, but rather that greater costs and effort are required to counter the vulnerability. (Indeed, the vastly increased costs of counterinsurgency in South Vietnam since 1962 are in part a reflection of the value of the eastern section of Laos, which shares a long border with North and South Vietnam. Following the Geneva accords, that ostensibly "neutralized" Laos in the summer of 1962, the Pathet Lao acquired effective control over this corridor—the so-called "Ho Chi Minh trail"—into South Vietnam. The result was to facilitate immensely North Vietnam's support for the Viet Cong insurgency, and to raise the costs of counterinsurgency in the south.)

The military value of Laos in some contingencies may alter according to the assumption that is made about the appropriate United States response—and more particularly about whether the appropriate response employs nuclear or conventional weapons. If Chinese intervention were sufficiently overt and massive that a quick nuclear response against the attacking force or against China itself was considered appropriate and feasible, then the value of Laos would be small. Whenever different United States responses are possible and when their effect on the military value of a country is likely to be

---

[2] My personal judgment is that both the contingencies referred to would require that large costs be incurred by the United States and the free world after the loss of Laos in order to maintain equivalent expected outcomes.

great, the alternatives must be weighed by estimating the probability of each of the different responses. With a nuclear response, for example, the derived value of Laos might be low, whereas in the case of a conventional response the derived value might be high. The *total* military value would be the sum of the separate values arising from each response weighted by the probability of its occurrence, if we could estimate it.[3] Thus, if the probability of a nuclear response were considered to be high, the total military value of Laos would be small. In the absence of such probability weights, we would have to look at all the relevant scenarios, note the value of Laos that emerges in each of the scenarios, and recognize that the largest of the resulting values is the maximum military value of Laos.

The same analytical framework might be used to answer the question of the military value of other Asian countries individually, or of all Southeast Asia (including Thailand, Vietnam, Burma, Malaya, and Indonesia) taken together. To evaluate the entire area, one might consider a scenario that includes the loss of the entire mainland area, and local wars involving, for example, the Philippines, India, Taiwan, or Australia. For contingencies involving island countries such as the Philippines, Taiwan, or Australia, the costs of maintaining equivalent military effectiveness would probably not be substantial. Island countries are already exposed to infiltration or invasion from the mainland to an extent that is unlikely to be increased as a result of the loss of other mainland areas. However, if Indonesia were lost, the incremental costs of maintaining equivalent security in Australia would be substantial, because of its increased exposure to air attack and the shorter supply lines that an Indonesian-based invasion force could draw on. In the case of the Philippines, the loss of Indonesia would require some additional costs in order to keep infiltration into Mindanao and the Sulu Archipelago to a constant level, but in general such incremental costs would be relatively modest. On the other hand, for countries such as India and Pakistan, whose accessible land borders (with Burma) would be extended by the loss of Southeast Asia, the incremental costs of maintaining equivalent defensibility might be appreciable.

[3] I am indebted to RAND consultant Robert Dorfman for making this point explicit.

This approach can be readily extended to evaluate the military worth of other countries and regions in the third world, particularly in the context of local nonnuclear wars. However, general nuclear wars present a very different picture. In general nuclear war, as distinct from local nonnuclear war, the value of most of the third world is minor. Of all the underdeveloped countries, those whose value in a general war context would probably be the greatest are in Latin America. For example, we might envisage a scenario with communist nuclear missile sites in Cuba, Mexico, and the Dominican Republic. In this situation the United States would have to ascertain the incremental costs of maintaining military security under these conditions equivalent to its posture in the absence of hostile missile bases. Such costs would involve the increased requirements for protecting retaliatory capabilities against an enemy first strike employing weapons of higher accuracy (and with less warning time) that could be delivered from such forward basing.[4] If the United States objective in such a war were to maintain a constant level of assured destruction against valued targets in the enemy's homeland, these incremental costs (for hardening, dispersal, or additional missiles) might be consequential. (On the other hand, if the United States objective were to strike first against the adversary's nuclear forces or, more likely, were to limit the damage he could cause to us in a gradually developing conflict, a basing posture in which the adversary's missiles were located in Latin America might actually be *preferred* by the United States.)

In a general war scenario, the primary value of Southeast Asia is its relation to targets that might be assigned to Air Force strategic forces based in or staging through the area. Inasmuch as these targets can be reached from other bases, or with other weapon systems (such as Polaris) not having such basing requirements, without entailing

---

[4] It is worth mentioning two other types of military value that some of the less-developed countries have in the general war context. The first concerns the role of foreign bases for aerial reconnaissance to obtain information about Soviet or Chinese weapons tests and other military activities. The loss of rights or facilities in areas near the Sino-Soviet periphery would entail substantially increased costs to the United States if equivalent information were to be obtained through other means. Conversely, Soviet acquisition of "listening posts" in countries close to the United States, such as Cuba, would result in better intelligence about United States rocket testing and related matters. To offset such benefits to the Soviet Union would impose additional costs on the United States.

heavy incremental costs, the value of the region in general war is small. And even this small value is declining with time and with the development of more-advanced weapon systems. Presumably a perception of this fact lies behind such views as those expressed in an influential report on Southeast Asia by a Senate group headed by Senator Mansfield in 1963. In effect, the Mansfield group tentatively concluded that perhaps the military significance of Southeast Asia had been exaggerated, and that "a thorough assessment of our own overall security requirements" might very well show that "an orderly curtailment of U.S. programs and missions in Southeast Asia need not pose a significant increase in the threat to our national security."[5]

Although this view makes sense if we think of national security interests in relation to *major nuclear* conflicts, it would be a mistake to conclude that the military value of Southeast Asia is small in all relevant military contingencies, including nonnuclear conflicts in adjacent areas. Indeed, as suggested above, the value of Southeast Asia and of individual Southeast Asian countries in some contingencies is probably quite large. The United States is a world power with military commitments, allies, and interests in areas remote from its strategic bases at home and abroad. As such we are concerned with the effect of major changes in the political and military orientation of areas such as Southeast Asia on the defensibility of adjacent areas. We are, for example, concerned with the effect of a change in the status of Laos on the costs of defending and securing Thailand and South Vietnam, and we would be concerned with the effect on the defense of India and Australia (as well as on the whole balance of forces in the Far East) of a loss of Southeast Asia, or of a change in the status of a major country in the area, such as Indonesia or Vietnam.

Of course, the question can legitimately be asked: Why should these United States interests and commitments in remote areas arise and why should they be maintained? Why can't they be pared without detriment to our fundamental national security posture? If an

---

[5] United States Senate, *Vietnam and Southeast Asia*, Report, Committee on Foreign Relations, 88th Congress, First Session, Washington, D. C., 1963, pp. 19-20.

invulnerable nuclear capability no longer requires forward basing of weapon systems in foreign countries, and if aerial surveillance of the Soviet Union and China can be adequately provided in the short run from a small number of foreign bases, or in the longer run from space satellites, why can't we retrench our foreign commitments in accordance with the reduced importance of these countries for the military security of the United States?

The answers to these questions are political, historical, and ideological, rather than military, and will be discussed later. But a few comments should be made here that relate to the indirect *military* value that the third world has for the United States.

American involvement in foreign areas has many explanations. In part, it is simply a historical legacy built on prior associations and on the relationships developed in the course of fighting wars and reconstructing after them. American commitments in Western Europe and Latin America, as well as in the Philippines and Korea, are cases in point. But involvement arises for contemporary as well as historical reasons. It arises, perhaps most fundamentally, as an inevitable reflection of the size, activity, and power of the United States. One of the inherent characteristics of modern national power is an abundance of expansive activities that intersect at many points with the interests and activities of other countries. These involvements arise in the day-to-day conduct of private as well as public affairs in trade, investment, travel, scientific research, education, journalism, foreign aid, diplomacy, and the dealings of international organizations. In some cases, the contacts develop into formal and explicit commitments, usually as a result of two influences: the existence of an immediate or anticipated threat or danger to particular countries; and a belief by American policymakers that some foreign political leaders, institutions, systems, and options are congenial to American values, while others are hostile. Under these influences, Presidents, Secretaries of State, and ambassadors convert the day-to-day contacts into more explicit forms of involvement with individual countries like Japan, and groups of countries like those in the Central Treaty Organization (CENTO), and the Southeast Asia Treaty Organization (SEATO).

The point of these observations does not necessarily rest on endorsement or even on acceptance of all the commitments that the United States has evolved. No doubt some are more sensible than others, and some may be quite misguided and inappropriate. Some commitments ought probably not to have been made. Some may have been bad bets to start with, and some could be pared without damage to the basic military security of the United States. The damage would be not to the military security of the United States, but to the contacts and activities, the historical continuity, and the values and integrity which engendered the commitments in the first place.[6]

From the standpoint of the military value of third-world areas, the point is that once such commitments have been made, the countries concerned, as well as neighboring countries, acquire military importance through the alternative-cost route already discussed. This is a good reason for being circumspect before making new commitments. But it is also a good reason for recognizing that the era of nuclear weaponry, stable deterrence, and invulnerable second-strike capabilities does not eliminate, and in certain circumstances actually enhances, the military worth of the third world to the United States.

ECONOMIC VALUE

There are two principal economic aspects of a country's value to the United States: the value of investments owned by American residents in the country; and the net value of (or "gains" from) trade with the country. As in the case of military values, the economic components can be approached in terms of the forgone benefits (or opportunity costs) of the hypothetically lost investments, imports, and exports. (However, it should be noted that loss in a military context does not necessarily imply loss in an economic sense. A country might become

---

[6] A similar point is made in the British Defence White Paper of 1965. After recognizing that "the only direct threat to our survival would be a major nuclear war arising from a direct conflict between East and West," the White Paper considers the need for forces and commitments in third-world areas.

These countries are rightly determined not to accept foreign domination; *but if our friends turn to us for help* we must be ready to give it where we can, so that they may achieve security and the chance to flourish in peace. (Italics added)

From The British Defence White Paper, February 1965, extracts published in *Survival*, The Institute of Strategic Studies, March-April 1965, p. 90.

a communist country, or a communist military base, and still continue to trade with the free world. Conversely, a country might expropriate foreign assets and forgo trading with the United States while still refusing to permit communist military installations on its territory.)

The value of American investments in a particular area is the discounted value of the income stream associated with them. In simpler language, the value of an asset is the earnings that are expected to be derived from it. The more distant the time in which the earnings are expected to accrue, the less they are worth in the present; that is, future earnings must be discounted to give them a present value, and the sum of these discounted present values is the value of the asset.

Though the concept is fairly clear, measurement is quite difficult because of the uncertainty connected with the income stream and with the appropriate discount rate to use in calculating present value. However, as a practical matter, the value of American investments in particular foreign areas might be assessed by taking the average income received in the last four or five years as a basis for estimating the income stream over, say, a twenty-year useful life, and by calculating present values by using three or four alternative, but plausible, discount rates. Alternatively, and still more simply, this component of value might be quantified by making a suitable upward adjustment in the book value of American assets in particular countries or areas. As an indication of the orders of magnitude that are involved here, the following figures on United States private direct investments abroad in 1959 are of interest:[7]

	($ BILLION)
Latin America	8.2
Europe	5.3
Africa	0.8
Asia (excluding the Middle East)	1.0
Middle East	1.2
Canada	10.2
Other	3.0
Total	29.7

[7] *U.S. Business Investments in Foreign Countries*, U.S. Department of Commerce, Washington, D. C., 1960, p. 92.

These figures are, of course, understated by perhaps 25 to 50 per cent because they reflect book value rather than market value. (They are also understated, from the standpoint of the "value" problem, because they do not include the value of European investments in, say, the Far East and the Middle East, which are frequently greater than those of the United States but which are also of indirect value to the United States.)

The value of a country or area as a source of United States imports is not equivalent to the total value of imports from that area. Imports obviously have to be paid for, and the loss of imports from an area also means that the payment is saved. On the other hand, a withdrawal of one country's exports from world markets usually will raise prices paid by the United States on imports of the same commodities from other sources. In a rough sense, the net gains from United States imports from a particular area can be approximated by the *difference* between what we currently pay and what we would have to pay if the imports were to be bought from the next-best sources.[8]

In the case of Southeast Asia, for instance, we can roughly approximate the maximum value of United States imports by considering what change might occur in the prices of, say, tin and copra, if Southeast Asia were to direct its trade entirely toward the communist bloc (a circumstance that would not necessarily follow from absorption of Southeast Asia into the communist bloc). Although Southeast Asia is a major world supplier of both these commodities, we would have to examine the elasticity of supply from *other* countries in order to get some notion of the change in prices that would result from a change in Southeast Asia's political status. In the absence of such examination, it can be safely said that the net value of imports from Southeast Asia (roughly estimated as the increase in prices that would result multiplied by the quantity of imports that would be affected) would be small in comparison with the total magnitude of United States imports from Southeast Asia.

To give a rough idea of the figures involved, United States imports

[8] More precisely, the value of these imports is the loss of consumer's surplus resulting from the higher import prices and reduced import volume.

in 1962 from the less-developed areas[9] were $5.8 billion, or 37 per cent of total imports of $15.8 billion.[10] Imports from all the less-developed countries by the United States plus Canada, Western Europe, Australia, New Zealand, South Africa, and Japan were about $20.8 billion, or 23 per cent of their total imports of $91.4 billion in 1962. Of this total, about $3.8 billion was provided from the area of South and Southeast Asia, including India, Pakistan, and Ceylon as well as Singapore, Malaysia (*i.e.*, Malaya, Sabah, and Sarawak), Indonesia, Laos, the Philippines, Thailand, Burma, Vietnam, and Cambodia.[11] United States imports from South and Southeast Asia were approximately $1.1 billion.

The concept of net value applies to exports as well as imports. The value of a particular area or country as a market for United States exports is not the total value of the exports themselves. In general, exports have an alternative, though less favorable, outlet; hence, the net value or gains from exporting to a particular area can be approximated by the expected *fall* in United States export prices that would result from such a shift in market outlet, multiplied by the quantity of exports that would be affected.[12] (Again, a change in the political orientation of the area toward the communist bloc does not necessarily imply that the area will cease to be an export market for the United States.)

To get some idea of the value of a particular country or area as an export market would require examination of the elasticity of demand for United States exports in *other* markets. In the absence of such an examination, I would conjecture that Southeast Asia's value as an export market for the United States would be small, although its value as an export market would probably be large for our European allies.

[9] Defined as all other nations except Canada, Western Europe, Australia, New Zealand, Japan, South Africa, and the Sino-Soviet bloc.

[10] United Nations, *Yearbook of International Trade Statistics, 1963*, New York, 1965, pp. 20–29.

[11] United Nations, *Economic Survey of Asia and the Far East*, New York, 1964, pp. 250–255.

[12] More precisely, the value of these exports is the loss of producer's surplus resulting from the lower export prices and reduced export volume.

To give a rough idea of the orders of magnitude involved, exports by the United States in 1962 to the less-developed areas of Asia, Africa, the Middle East, and Latin America were $7 billion or about 33 per cent of total exports of $21.4 billion.[13] Exports to the less-developed areas, excluding communist countries, by the United States plus Canada, Western Europe, Australia, New Zealand, South Africa, and Japan were $21.2 billion in 1962, or about 22 per cent of their total exports of $94.5 billion. Exports by these countries to South and Southeast Asia amounted to $5.2 billion. United States exports to South and Southeast Asia were about $1.6 billion.

To move from these aggregate figures to specific estimates of the economic value of particular countries to the United States would require extensive empirical work. But the concepts are clear, and with some reasonable simplifying assumptions, it should not be too difficult to make acceptable quantitative estimates for the economic, as well as military, aspects of value.

However, the magnitude of a country's military and economic value to the United States does not necessarily imply that we should be willing to incur costs equivalent to this value in order to prevent the loss of the country. Before taking this step, we should have to have some assurance that incurring such costs would reduce the likelihood that the loss would take place anyhow. Thus, all that the quantitative components of a country's value tell us is the *maximum* cost we should be willing to incur to reduce the likelihood that a still more costly alternative might occur.

Furthermore, we do not imply that the United States should undertake an economic or military aid program in a particular country just because the costs of the aid program are less than the value of the country. Of course, we should certainly not undertake aid programs that would cost *more* than this value. However, to know how close to this maximum we ought to go, it is necessary to estimate how high the probability would remain, if the aid programs were undertaken, that the loss of the country in question would occur anyhow, over the particular time period that concerns us. It should be intui-

[13] United Nations, *Yearbook of International Trade Statistics, 1963, op. cit.*, pp. 20–29.

tively clear that the higher the residual probability that within this period the country would collapse anyway (or, put another way, that the aid programs would not be effective in accomplishing their objective), the less justifiable it would be to incur the costs of additional aid. In other words, before being able to say whether the costs of a particular aid program, economic or military, are justified, we should consider not just the value of the country in which the program is undertaken, but the probable *effectiveness* of the program as well.[14] Later chapters will return to the question of which effects seem reasonable to expect from economic and military aid programs and which do not, and the bearing of these effects on United States program objectives.[15]

NONQUANTITATIVE COMPONENTS OF VALUE

The problem of value is further complicated by the highly important political and psychological components. Indeed, consideration of these components may appreciably raise the costs that we are prepared to incur to reduce the probability of the loss of a country.

[14] Consider a program (for example, economic or military aid) costing X. Associated with X is a probability of loss, P. In the absence of X, the probability of loss is estimated as π, with $\pi > P$. Assuming the value of the country concerned is V, X is justifiable only if:

$$X + PV < \pi V, \quad \text{or} \tag{1a}$$
$$X < V(\pi - P). \tag{1b}$$

In the case most favorable for the contemplated program, π is close to one and P is close to zero. Hence, $(\pi - P)$ approaches unity, and V provides the upper bound for a justifiable X. Generally, however, $(\pi - P)$ will be less than unity, because P will seldom approach zero. Hence, *a justifiable X ought to be appreciably less than* V.

It is easy to adapt this formulation to allow for the fact that if "no loss" occurs, with or without X, some further costs may subsequently have to be incurred to support the country under consideration. Under this circumstance, X will be less attractive the greater the subsequent "no-loss" costs are likely to be. Denoting these subsequent costs by S, (1a) and (1b) can be restated:

$$X + PV + (1 - P)S < V\pi + (1 - \pi)S, \quad \text{or} \tag{2a}$$
$$X < V(\pi - P) + S(P - \pi). \tag{2b}$$

In this case a justifiable X must be less in relation to V than in the preceding case, because additional costs will be required after X, since $P - \pi < 0$.

[15] See pp. 21–22 and 82–86 below, and Chapters Six and Seven.

As previously mentioned, some—and perhaps most—political and psychological values are nonquantitative. This does not mean that a serious attempt to fill in the numbers should not be made where possible. But it does mean that the qualitative aspects must be borne prominently in mind before reaching a conclusion on the basis of the economic and military components alone.

One important qualitative consideration arises from the reasonable premise, noted earlier, that the United States has an ideological preference for the emergence in the less-developed areas of relatively free, open, and democratic societies. If the premise itself is questioned, the answer can be given that these characteristics are valued because they are likely to be associated with a world in which diversity and mobility flourish, and in which the quality of life is more rewarding. Such reasoning suggests that there are important ideological components of value, but, as indicated earlier, this does not enable us to think quantitatively about them. Quantitative estimates of ideological dimensions of value must be waived in favor of qualitative judgments and intuitions.

A second major qualitative consideration concerns the political-psychological interdependencies among countries and areas. Some of these (for example, between Laos on the one hand, and Vietnam and Thailand on the other) can be identified in military or economic terms, costed, and offset or simply accepted. But there are other interdependencies characterized by attitudes that are expressed in phrases like "wave of the future" or "march of history" or "inevitable trend," that cannot be readily offset or accepted. In other words, there is a psychological dimension to the "domino" effect which can exceed as well as reinforce the military and logistic dimensions discussed earlier. Attempts can be made to compensate for the military and economic consequences of a particular country's loss, but it is more difficult to find ways to compensate for the effect of a dimly perceived notion of "trend" on the loyalties and confidence of other people and countries. Although these political-psychological interdependencies exist particularly among countries of the third world, they extend beyond. We would be wrong to think that the loss of such a country as India might not have nearly as profound a psychological impact on the United Kingdom and Western Europe, as, for example, the loss of Laos would have on confidence and loyalties in Thailand and South Vietnam; or that the loss of South Korea might not have an equivalent impact on Japan.

Clearly, individual countries can acquire a symbolic political value which exceeds their actual economic and military importance. There is, in fact, probably no better indicator of the symbolic political importance that countries acquire than the extent of a prior United States commitment, whether formal or tacit, to assure the country's viability and independence from communist control. United States commitments may be signified by formal guarantee, as in the case of the SEATO countries, but they may also be signified more informally by large military aid programs or by substantial amounts of nonmilitary aid, as in the case of India. In such cases, a country's importance to the United States will exceed that which can be measured simply by looking at the economic and military components of value.

Although it is a standard precept of economics to ignore costs that have been previously expended, or "sunk," in deciding whether or not to undertake a new investment, in this particular context sunk costs may be quite relevant. To the extent that such prior costs have signaled to other countries that the United States has placed great value on the integrity of a particular country, the repercussions that would ensue from the loss of the country will be enlarged. In this sense, prior costs and prior policies may have the effect of inflating the political value of a country beyond its quantitative economic and military values. As a world power with military commitments, allies, and interests abroad, the United States must be concerned with the effect of major changes in the political and military orientation of particular countries on the credibility and confidence with which other countries regard United States commitments in the future.

The value of other countries in relation to the character of the United States domestic society is more tenuous and certainly more difficult to measure, but not necessarily less important. If any major group of countries were to turn communist, one consequence of their loss would probably be a rise in the United States defense budget, including that part devoted to foreign military assistance, and per-haps—though less likely—a drop in the real national product as well as in its rate of growth. Notwithstanding some prophets of gloom, a 20 per cent, or a 50 per cent, or even a 200 per cent increase in the size of the defense budget would not "bankrupt" the United States, nor would a 2 per cent annual rate of growth in national product, rather than a 5 per cent growth rate, mean national doom. But it is probably fair to say that substantially increased defense budgets main-tained over a protracted period, if associated with a relatively slow rate of growth in the economy, would have some significant effects on the character and quality of the domestic society—on the extent of bureaucracy, on the control of information, on the sense of ten-sion and vigilance in daily living.

If we consider, further, various extreme contingencies concerning the progressive erosion of the free world, it might ultimately become extremely difficult to determine where the "iron curtain" began and where it ended. A progressive reduction in the area of the world in which we could freely travel would significantly curtail our freedom, quite apart from the effect of such insulation on the quality of do-mestic society in the United States. In effect, under such extreme contingencies, the iron curtain would become something around *us*, rather than around the Soviet bloc or China.

Finally, a world of such a piecemeal and sequential erosion would be one in which new generations of Americans would face increasing temptations to affiliate with the trend rather than oppose it. An in-ward-directed and withdrawn America might generate its own do-mestic opponents with an increasing disposition to overturn it from within.

CONCLUSIONS

It is possible to think in quantitative terms about some components of the "value" of particular countries to the United States, but not about other components. The military and economic components of value seem most amenable to quantitative treatment, whereas the political and psychological components are least amenable.

Viewed in terms of alternative costs, the military value of the less-developed countries is generally highest in nonnuclear conflicts in adjacent areas, and quite low in nuclear wars among the major powers. Latin America is a partial exception to this generalization because missiles based in Latin American countries might expose the United States to an increased risk of surprise attack.

The economic value of the less-developed countries to the United States will vary depending on their trade patterns and on the availability of alternative markets for United States exports and of imports from other sources of supply. It is very likely that the economic value of particular countries in the third world will be greater for American allies in Western Europe and Japan than for the United States itself.

The political-psychological value of particular countries in the third world is least amenable to an alternative-cost estimating technique. At the least, it seems fair to say that the indirect political-psychological importance of certain underdeveloped areas is likely to be very great from the standpoint of effects on Western Europe and Japan in particular, and these effects in turn would have an appreciable impact on attitudes and expectations in the United States and on the character of the domestic society in the long run.

Though these points are inconclusive, they have some bearing on United States objectives in the third world. The analysis suggests that the United States should be primarily interested in strengthening the independence of the less-developed countries and their freedom from foreign domination, as well as in advancing their mutual efforts to protect themselves. The importance of most of these areas for general deterrence purposes, or in the event of nuclear war with the Soviet Union or with China, is negligible. And, in fact, the value of most of these areas to the United States will be protected so long as their independence from Soviet or Chinese communist control is secure. If this important condition is satisfied, a wide range of internal and foreign policies in the third world would be entirely consistent with United States interests and objectives. Whether a country calls itself "neutralist" or "allied," and whether it relies primarily on public or private enterprise for advancing its economic development are questions of fundamentally secondary concern to the United States compared with the questions of whether a country is taking the internal and external measures that contribute to strengthening its independence from external and internal communist domination. In this sense, the *denial* of communist control in the third world is probably the primary objective of American foreign policy in these areas.

Besides the objective of denial, the United States also has a set of *development* objectives that spring from a preference for open, progressive, and accessible societies in the rest of the world. Economic growth and social advancement are important aspects of these aims. But the denial objective is primary. It should, moreover, provide a powerful link between the value of the third world to the United States and the interests of these countries themselves in strengthening the foundations of their own independence.

CHAPTER TWO

Connections Between Political, Economic, and Military Problems

If the various aspects of "value" discussed in the previous chapter comprise the stakes, the circumstances and relationships prevailing in the third world determine the problems and set the constraints confronting United States policies. Quite apart from the value of the less-developed countries, these relationships affect what American policies and programs can reasonably aspire to accomplish.

It is trite but true to observe that generalizing about the less-developed areas is hazardous; conditions vary widely from country to country. With this caution in mind, we will examine some of the generalizations that have been made, raise some questions about them, and suggest a few other generalizations that are often overlooked or insufficiently stressed. We will first be concerned with connections between economic development and political development, and then consider relationships between military factors on the one hand, and the process of economic and political development on the other.

ECONOMIC DEVELOPMENT
AND POLITICAL INSTITUTIONS

There are many different and often conflicting hypotheses concerning the political effects of economic conditions and programs. Our aim here is not to review all these hypotheses but rather to reflect the diversity among them.

ECONOMIC DEVELOPMENT AND DEMOCRACY

According to one widespread view, economic growth tends to prevent authoritarianism and to promote stable democratic political institutions. Testifying in support of the 1958 foreign aid program, Secretary of State Dulles reflected this view:

> Today millions of people in these [less-developed] countries seek the answer to this simple question: Do political independence and freedom mean economic growth? If these peoples do not feel that in freedom they get growth, then freedom will be on its way out in much of the world. These people are determined to move forward. If they do not succeed there will be increasing discontent which may sweep away their moderate leaders of today and bring to power extremist leaders who will resort to extremist measures fostered by international communism.[1]

A similar view was expressed by Secretary Rusk, testifying in support of the same program five years later:

> Our own interest requires us to assist those who are threatened by the domination of others. In the developing nations of the world a sound growing economy provides forward momentum and hope—those essential elements which will lessen the temptation to grasp at quick authoritarian routes to progress and possible external domination.[2]

While social scientists tend to be more circumspect, they often

[1] United States Senate, *Mutual Security Act of 1957*, Hearings, Committee on Foreign Relations, 85th Congress, First Session, Washington, D. C., 1957, pp. 4–5.

[2] United States Senate, *Foreign Assistance Act of 1963*, Hearings, Committee on Foreign Relations, 88th Congress, First Session, Washington, D. C., 1963, p. 7.

convey an essentially similar position. Thus, in 1957 Max Millikan and Walt Rostow asserted:

> Under modern circumstances some improvement in the standard of living, while not enough by itself, is certainly a necessary condition for the development of stable and peaceful societies and for the survival of democratic institutions.[3]

In recent years, both official and academic statements have frequently viewed the connection between economic development and democratic political development in more guarded and indirect terms. Stress has been placed instead on the link between economic development and the maintenance of national independence, but the outcome is the same. As Edward Mason has suggested:

> Favorable prospects for economic development have significant relevance for the ability of countries to maintain their independence. . . . In most of the underdeveloped world . . . the problem essentially is to keep open the possibility, and to encourage the unfolding of a process of economic and political development that offers a real alternative to Communism.[4]

In a world in which loss of national independence is often synonymous with communist control, and communism is implicitly considered to be irreversible, prospects for democratic development depend on maintaining national independence. Consequently, if independence depends on economic growth, then democratic development also depends on economic growth, although the relationship is indirect.

Moreover, there is some evidence to support these views, if we concentrate on long-term relationships, neglecting short-term effects. Several competent studies by political scientists, sociologists, and economists have suggested that a positive relationship exists between a ranking of countries in accordance with the level of economic development, and their ranking in accordance with the "competitive-

[3] Max F. Millikan and W. W. Rostow, *A Proposal: Key to an Effective Foreign Policy*, New York, Harper & Bros., 1957, p. 25.

[4] Edward S. Mason, *Foreign Aid and Foreign Policy*, New York, Harper and Row, 1964, p. 51.

ness" of politics.[5] The main result was that "there is a positive correlation between economic development and political competitiveness."[6] The several studies yielded equivalent results, and also suggested that the relationship holds true among the Latin American, the Asian, and the African regions. Tables 2-1 and 2-2 reproduce the results of one of these studies.

Although all the studies indicate a positive relationship between political and economic factors, it should be noted that the results are not sufficiently uniform to suggest a powerful relationship. Chapter Six will reconsider the strength of this relationship using more detailed data and other analytical techniques.

In addition to this type of empirical evidence, the examples of precommunist Kuomintang China and of India since its independence in 1947 provide additional (but perhaps not less important or less influential) evidence of a connection between economic and political development. In the five years between the end of World War II and the victory of the Chinese Communists on the Mainland, the Chinese economy was severely afflicted by inflation, stagnation, and acute poverty under the Nationalist Chinese government. The "lesson" that was drawn from the China experience seemed to be that these economic factors played a decisive role in bringing about the

---

[5] See, for example, Seymour Lipset, "Some Social Requisites of Democracy: Economic Development and Political Legitimacy," *American Political Science Review*, Vol. 53, No. 1, March 1959, pp. 69–105; James S. Coleman, "The Political Systems of the Developing Areas," in G. A. Almond and J. S. Coleman (eds.), *The Politics of the Developing Areas*, Princeton, Princeton University Press, 1960; and Everett E. Hagen, Ch. 1, "A Framework for Analyzing Economic and Political Change," in Asher, Hagen, *et al.*, *Development of the Emerging Countries*, Washington, D. C., The Brookings Institution, 1962. The ranking according to level of economic development was based on a simple aggregation of separate indexes of welfare (GNP per person and doctors per 1,000 people); communications development (vehicles, telephones, radios, and newspaper circulation per 1,000 or 10,000 population); industrialization (energy consumption per capita, and per cent of labor force employed outside agriculture and service sectors); urbanization (proportion of population in cities over 100,000); and education (proportion of population estimated to be literate and primary-school enrollment in proportion to school-age population). Political competitiveness or openness was judged in terms of the extent to which many groups have an opportunity to articulate their views and interests and to participate in and influence political decision making.
[6] Coleman, in Almond and Coleman, *op. cit.*, p. 538.

TABLE 2-1 *Classification of Less-Developed Countries by Type of Political Structure and Rank in Economic Development: Latin America*

RANK IN ECONOMIC DEVELOPMENT	COMPETITIVENESS OF POLITICAL STRUCTURE		
	COMPETITIVE	SEMICOMPETITIVE	AUTHORITARIAN
1	Argentina		
2	Uruguay		
3	Venezuela		
4			Cuba
5	Chile		
6		Panama	
7		Mexico	
8	Costa Rica		
9		Colombia	
10	Brazil		
11			Paraguay
12		Peru	
13		Ecuador	
14			Dominican Republic
15			Nicaragua
16			El Salvador
17			Bolivia
18		Guatemala	
19			Honduras
20			Haiti

Source: Everett E. Hagen, "A Framework for Analyzing Economic and Political Change," in Asher, Hagen, *et al., Development of the Emerging Countries,* Washington, D. C., The Brookings Institution, 1962, p. 4. The data are from the 1956–1960 period.

erosion of support for the Nationalist government, and the growth of support for communist authoritarianism.[7]

In India, the country's planned economic development has been so vital among the objectives of democratic government that its success has been plausibly viewed as necessary for the success, and indeed the survival, of democracy. The view that democracy is on trial

[7] For discussion of the lesson of China and its bearing on the relative merits and importance of economic and military aid programs, see Charles Wolf, Jr., *Foreign Aid: Theory and Practice in Southern Asia,* Princeton, Princeton University Press, 1960, pp. 40-43 ff. (hereafter referred to as "Wolf, *Foreign Aid*").

TABLE 2-2   *Classification of Less-Developed Countries by Type of Political Structure and Rank in Economic Development: Asia and Africa*

RANK IN ECONOMIC DEVELOPMENT	COMPETITIVENESS OF POLITICAL STRUCTURE		
	COMPETITIVE	SEMICOMPETITIVE	AUTHORITARIAN
1	Lebanon		
2	Malaya		
3			United Arab Republic
4	Philippines		
5	Turkey		
6			Iraq
7	Ceylon		
8		Morocco	
9		Jordan	
10		Tunisia	
11			Libya
12		Ghana	
13			Iran
14		Thailand	
15		Indonesia	
16	India		
17		Malagasy Republic	
18			Saudi Arabia
19		Burma	
20		Cambodia	
21		Cameroons	
22		South Vietnam	
23		Nigeria	
24			Pakistan
25			Laos
26			Liberia
27			Sudan
28		Togoland	
29			Ethiopia
30			Afghanistan

Source: Everett E. Hagen, "A Framework for Analyzing Economic and Political Change," in Asher, Hagen, *et al.*, *Development of the Emerging Countries*, Washington, D. C., The Brookings Institution, 1962, p. 2. The data are from the 1956–1960 period.

in India, and that the judgment rendered will depend heavily on economic performance, is admittedly oversimplified. But there is enough truth in it to make it realistic and relevant. In effect, the Indian and Chinese "lessons" are the affirmative and negative versions of the same hypothesis: economic development is essential (though not sufficient) for the survival of democracy; lacking effective economic performance, an inchoate democratic system is likely to perish.

Although the Indian and Chinese "lessons" supplement the studies of politico-economic relationships, there is a basic difference between these two forms of evidence. The cited studies are concerned with the relationship between political *level* and economic development *level*, while the evidence from India and China is concerned with the relationship between economic and political *changes*. If the relationships suggested by the Indian and Chinese examples hold true, we would expect that, in the long run, political and economic levels would be associated: Democratic states would have higher levels of economic development because they would not survive as democracies if they did not sustain satisfactory growth. However, the relationship between political and economic levels might exist *without* the short-run connection implied by the examples of India and China. In the short run, economic development might strain and even disrupt new and weak democracies, but in the long run such development might be necessary for the loosening of centralized controls and the emergence (or re-emergence) of democracy. The comparison of levels of political and economic development suggests nothing about the *process* of arriving at the levels. In contrast, the Indian and Chinese cases are presumed to suggest something about the process through which political development level is maintained or changed.

The political implications of classical economics also link economic and political development, but the influences that are presumed to be at work are very different. Arising as a reaction against mercantilism in the eighteenth century, classical economics regarded economic growth as dependent on the freedom and initiative of private enterprise and on the removal of state monopolies, tolls, and other governmental interferences with the free market. A breakdown of centralized controls was thus considered essential for growth. The link between economic freedom and political democracy lay in the further argument that a reduction of central government powers and controls would also widen opportunities for individual liberty and political pluralism. A latter-day classicist, Milton Friedman, expresses this view as follows:

> Central government control would be a poor way to promote economic development. What is required is rather an atmosphere of freedom, of maximum opportunity for individuals to experiment, and of incentive for them to do so in an environment in which there are objective tests of success and failure—in short, a vigorous free capitalistic market.

Moreover, this process is connected with the emergence and survival of democracy:

> Democracy and freedom have never been either attained or maintained except in communities in which the bulk of economic activity is organized through private enterprise.[8]

Another line of theorizing, with different policy implications, is concerned with the relationship between political change and the *distribution* of economic, political, and social opportunities and benefits. Current aid programs, such as the Alliance for Progress, stress reform, "social progress," and "social equity" as much as growth; they are based on implicit theorizing about the connections between distributive considerations on the one hand, and political evolution or revolution on the other. But the underlying perception goes back at least as far as Aristotle, who, in his discussion of the causes of revolution in Greece, stated:

> Everywhere inequality is a cause of revolution . . . and always it is the desire of equality which rises in rebellion.[9]

---

[8] Milton Friedman, "Foreign Economic Aid: Means and Objectives," *The Yale Review*, Vol. 47, No. 4, Summer 1958, pp. 504, 509. For similar views, see D. M. Wright's chapter on "Growth, Capitalism and Democracy" in his *Capitalism*, New York, McGraw-Hill, 1951, pp. 93–100. My own views on the Friedman position were set forth in "Economic Aid Reconsidered," *The Yale Review*, Vol. 50, No. 4, Summer 1961, pp. 518–532.

[9] Aristotle, *Politics*, New York, The Modern Library, 1943, p. 211.

Aristotle had in mind the inequality between what people have and what they think or feel is rightfully due them. Translated in terms of the modern scene, its implications are fairly clear. In an environment in which Western egalitarian ideologies and democratic constitutions are widespread, adherence to a vocabulary of political equality and representative institutional forms is pervasive, even when the forms are simply a facade. Under these circumstances, the persistence of large inequalities in wealth, income, and economic opportunities creates a deep current of grievance and discontent—a gnawing resentment arising from the gap between a desired equality and experienced inequality.

If there is a connection between this distributive theory and the theories that relate economic development to the survival of new democracies, it arises from the fact that redistributive measures may be easier to accomplish in growing than in stagnant economies. It may be easier to distribute *increases* in national income and wealth equitably than to attempt to redistribute existing income and wealth. Under these circumstances, we might expect to find a statistical association among economic growth, equitable distribution, and political democracy.

ECONOMIC DEVELOPMENT, REVOLUTION, AND AUTHORITARIANISM

These generalizations and theories are familiar and reassuring to most Americans; indeed, they have had a powerful influence on our thinking about the less-developed countries. However, there are other theories that contrast sharply with them. Nearly opposite views can be cited that assert an *inverse* relationship between economic and social development on the one hand, and democratic political development on the other.[10] Higher rates of economic development may lead to the breakdown of an existing social structure and to the end of prospects for evolutionary development toward more open and competitive institutions. Revolution may be the result, either accom-

---

[10] For an effective statement of these views, see Mancur Olson, Jr., "Rapid Growth as a Destabilizing Force," *Journal of Economic History*, Vol. 23, No. 4, December 1963, pp. 529–552.

panied by authoritarian control or followed by authoritarian reactions.

One of the most persuasive expressions of this view is De Tocqueville's analysis of the circumstances leading to the French Revolution. From his study of rural and urban statistics in prerevolutionary France, De Tocqueville's well-known conclusion was:

> . . . that in none of the decades immediately following the Revolution did our national prosperity make such rapid forward strides as in the two preceding it. . . . The fact remains that the country did grow richer and living conditions improved throughout the land.[11]

Nevertheless, he pointed out,

> It is a singular fact that this steadily increasing prosperity, far from tranquilizing the population, everywhere promoted a spirit of unrest. Moreover, those parts of France in which the improvement in the standard of living was most pronounced were the chief centers of the revolutionary movement. . . . It was precisely in those parts of France where there had been most improvement that popular discontent ran highest.[12]

Along similar lines, Crane Brinton concludes his study of the downfall of the old regimes in England, America, France, and Russia with the observation that:

> These were all societies . . . on the upgrade economically before the Revolution came, and the revolutionary movements seem to originate in the discontents of not unprosperous people who feel restraint, cramp, annoyance, rather than downright crushing oppression. Certainly these revolutions are not started by down-and-outers, by starving, miserable people.[13]

Eric Hoffer's trenchant observations on mass movements have a similar flavor:

> It is not actual suffering but the taste of better things which excites

[11] Alexis de Tocqueville, *The Old Regime and the French Revolution*, New York, Doubleday and Co., Inc., 1955, p. 174.

[12] *Ibid.*, pp. 175–176.

[13] Crane Brinton, *The Anatomy of Revolution*, New York, Vintage Books (rev. 1962), p. 64.

people to revolt. . . . Our frustration is greater when we have much and want more than when we have nothing and want some.[14]

As Hoffer notes, mass movements and the revolutions they generate may be good or bad, regenerative or restrictive. But under contemporary circumstances in many of the less-developed countries, communism unfortunately often appears as the most powerful candidate for leadership and control of mass movements. As a result, there may often be a disturbingly close connection between the occurrence of revolutionary movements and the probability of a communist takeover.

The standard Marxist interpretation of the revolutionary process is partly consistent with these views. In order to prepare the conditions needed for revolutionary overthrow of an existing society, communist ideology—or at least one branch of it—asserts that it is necessary to advance the level of development, specifically to industrialize, and thereby to create an urban proletariat. Economic development will bring prosperity only for a while and for the few. Thereafter the discontent and "immiserization" of the proletariat will provide support for the revolutionary movement. By intensifying the class struggle, economic development and industrialization play an essential role in the process of overthrowing existing institutions and supplanting them with the dictatorship of the proletariat.

Modern political sociology takes a more sophisticated view of the process, but it also suggests an inverse relationship between economic and political development. Thus, Edward Shils argues that:

> The process of economic development through governmental action is probably injurious to the stability of any political regime—not least, democratic regimes. . . . It seems inherent in economic development . . . for plans and expectations to exceed achievements, even when achievements are substantial. The new governments are ambitious for dramatic accomplishments and therefore they aim high; their inexperience causes them to over-plan and to fall short of their planned objectives. This creates stress within the elite . . . [which becomes] impatient of obstacles and fearful of criticism, [and] reluctant to see its plans and achievements subjected to de-

[14] Eric Hoffer, *The True Believer*, New York, Harper & Bros., 1952, p. 28.

tached criticism. . . . Thus, we may conclude that large-scale programs of economic development being undertaken in the new states do weaken the already weak foundations of political democracy and push in a more oligarchical direction.

Although the emphasis in the quotation is on *governmental* programs of economic development, Shils notes that:

> Even if comparable economic progress were made by other means, the results would still be disturbing to the traditional order . . . and toward political stability as well.[15]

Moreover, if we consider the evidence provided by recent political history, the communist revolution in Cuba suggests a different relationship between economic and political development from that we previously associated with India and Kuomintang China. Prior to 1958, per capita income in Cuba was among the five or six highest in Latin America; and economic conditions during 1956–1958 were generally good, although economic growth appeared to be slow. As Boris Goldenberg has observed, social and economic inequalities were probably less pronounced in Cuba than elsewhere in Latin America, and had diminished in recent decades. Moreover, Cuba's middle class appeared to be growing, and the Communist party was weak. Goldenberg concludes that:

> The Cuban revolution shows that a Communist-type revolution can be successful where there is no feudalism, little conscious misery, no general popular despair, no mass desire for a "socialist" transformation, and no strong Communist Party.[16]

It is evident that the views we have discussed are widely disparate. In some cases they conflict with one another; in others they represent different but not conflicting positions. For example, the view that there is a positive relationship between *level* of economic development and degree of political competitiveness does not conflict with the

---

[15] Edward Shils, *Political Development in the New States*, The Hague, Mouton and Co., 1962, pp. 27–28.
[16] Boris Goldenberg, "The Cuban Revolution: An Analysis," *Problems of Communism*, September–October 1962, pp. 2–3.

view that the *process* of economic and social development may be destabilizing and can lead to revolutionary political change and to oligarchic or dictatorial centralization of power. There may indeed be some tendency for higher levels of economic development to be associated with more open political institutions (although there are to many obvious counterexamples from the past generation—examples not confined to the Soviet Union—to make one confident of this tendency). Economic development may widen opportunities and stimulate the broad range of skills, interests, and communication which pluralistic societies require. Indeed, the Soviet Union may be undergoing some of these changes itself. But economic development may also forge new instruments of surveillance, manipulation, and centralized control. Whether the potential for democratic pluralism or for authoritarian centralism will predominate is not clear, nor are the circumstances in which one or the other may occur.

Moreover, even if sustained growth increases the prospects for pluralism more than for authoritarianism in the long run, the intermediate process of arriving at a higher level of economic development may be fraught with risks that embryonic democratic institutions will be destroyed and replaced by authoritarian institutions. Although democracy in India may not survive without economic development and modernization, the process of development may also create stresses and strains that jeopardize its survival. The web is tangled, and the risks from "too much" or "too little" or "not the right kind" of development are numerous and grave. Communism is only one possible outcome, as the experiences of the numerous Southeast Asian, Middle Eastern, and Latin American dictatorships illustrate. Communism is, however, unique in its assumed irreversibility, and for this reason—as well as others—it is the graver risk.[17]

[17] In an earlier study, I attempted to reconcile some of these differing political-economic relationships. The study expressed the degree of vulnerability or susceptibility to extremist political ideologies and institutions in terms of (1) the relationship between a number of socio-economic variables relating to economic *aspirations*, and (2) a number of other variables relating both to the level of living and to rates of change in the level of living as measures of economic *performance*.

The indicators of economic aspirations that were used involved literacy levels, educational expenditures, and frequency of contact with superior con-

THE ROLE OF FORCE

The realities in the underdeveloped areas are still more complex than our discussion suggests. Grievances, resentments, and frustrations are widely different in different countries, but abundant in all. Poverty, stagnation, discrimination, and distributional inequities are not only pervasive, but often become less tolerable because of the all-too-modest improvements that are accomplished. Hypersensitive nationalism may hinder effective external aid for internal programs of improvement and development. And ineffectual aid will almost surely intensify nationalistic resentment and hostility. Modest improvement often seems as likely to foment aggressiveness and dissatisfaction over the inadequacy of change as to allay the original grievances. It is important to mitigate these grievances. However, it is also important to recognize that there is probably an ineradicable minimum of grievances, which can be exploited by ingenuity, resources, and organization to challenge and sometimes to overturn even a relatively effective political system. Such recognition is essential for understanding and meeting insurgency in the third world, a subject which will be discussed in Chapter Three.[18]

What, then, are the implications of these views for United States policies and programs in the less-developed countries? Are economic development programs as likely to accentuate as to relieve the pent-up pressures that exist in these countries? Are military aid programs likely to assure the postponement of needed changes just long

---

sumption standards; the performance indicators with which these aspirations were compared consisted both of consumption levels and wage rates, and of rates of change in these variables. In a preliminary and crude test of the predictive value of the model, general variations in the proportion of communist votes received in the Indian national elections were used as an index of the susceptibility to extremist political solutions. The regional variations within India predicted by the model were found to correlate quite closely with the variation in communist voting proportions. See Wolf, *Foreign Aid*, pp. 296–351. Compare the results of this study, however, with the statement by Shils, above, that hypothesized that the gap between aspirations and performance in the process of economic development is inevitably going to widen because of the temptation of leaders to promise too much.

[18] See below, Chapter Three, especially pp. 50–54.

enough to make the eventual changes explosive and hostile to United States interests?

The candid answer to these questions is that we do not know enough about the differences between the processes of controlled change and explosive change to be able to predict confidently what the effects of our programs and policies will be. But certainly any endeavor to effect controlled change will involve the *responsible use of force*, combined with economic growth and modernization, and increased distributional equity. Generalizing from his study of revolutionary movements in England, the United States, France, and Russia, Brinton concludes:

> One is impressed in all four instances more with the ineptitude of the governments' use of force than with the skill of their opponents' use of force. It is almost safe to say that no government is likely to be overthrown until it loses the ability to make adequate use of its military and police powers. That loss of ability may show itself in the actual desertion of soldiers and police to the revolutionists, or in the stupidity with which the government manages its soldiers and police. . . .[19]

In an environment in which communist subversion and "liberation wars" are a constant threat, and the skills of subversion and guerrilla warfare have been highly developed, Brinton's statement warrants important additions. But the nature of such additions would probably be to strengthen the demands placed upon the use of force in the process of controlled political and social change.

The problem of maintaining and strengthening noncommunist political systems, and of enhancing prospects for a progressive expansion of pluralistic and democratic institutions, may be viewed as one of achieving a balance among the three factors discussed above: economic development, distributional equity, and the responsible use of force. However, the problem is made still more complicated by the fact that the appropriate balance is a changing one: the desirable combination of force, development, and redistribution will differ at different times and in different countries.

[19] Brinton, *The Anatomy of Revolution, op. cit.*, pp. 266–267.

The need for force arises from the threat of external aggression against some of the less-developed countries, and from the threat of internal subversion in most of them. The external threat is greatest in those countries on the Chinese periphery, notably Korea, Taiwan, Laos, Vietnam, Thailand, Burma, and India, although countries in the neighborhoods of Egypt, Algeria, Cuba, and perhaps Indonesia also face external threats. Elsewhere in Africa and Latin America, the external threat is of little consequence, although it cannot be ignored.

In general, however, the main threat is that of internal subversion, often combined with external logistic support, propaganda, and organization, and with direct pressure from external forces and bases. It would be as wrong to deny the important role of such external support (as Laos and Vietnam have demonstrated) as it would be to deny that the climate for successful subversion is also dependent on such internal factors as poverty, economic stagnation, governmental inefficiency, indecency, and corruption, and inequitable distribution of income, land, and opportunity. When, as is frequently the case, these conditions are combined with acute nationalism and with resentment against the West because of its present wealth and the real and fancied evils of colonialism in the past, the ingredients of successful subversion and "liberation wars" are readily available.

Although there will always be an ineradicable minimum of shortcomings and grievances that are subject to subversive exploitation, the further above this minimum actual conditions are, the lower will be the costs and the greater the ease of subversion in the less-developed countries. Conversely, the closer to the minimum actual conditions are, the higher will be the costs and the greater the difficulty of subversion. Both internal and external factors are important, and programs and policies designed to deal with them play an important role in United States policies toward developing countries.

Moreover, the interaction between internal and external factors in the process of subversion is not confined to countries on the Sino-Soviet periphery. Venezuela provides a case in point in Latin America. Communist terrorists using arms partly received from Cuba tried to disrupt the democratic regime of Romulo Betancourt and to prevent free presidential elections in December 1963. Venezuela's experience also illustrates the earlier point that governments undertaking effective programs of development, redistribution, and democratization are not immune to serious challenge from communist subversion. The key role of force in defeating such a challenge is suggested by the fact that Venezuela's per capita defense expenditures are the highest in Latin America.[20]

The usual distinction between military force and police force is made according to whether the force deals with external or internal threats. In the less-developed countries the relationship between the two types of force is often much closer than in the developed countries because the connections between external and internal aggression are often also close. Externally provided resources often furnish training and leadership cadres, materials, and sometimes combat units, whether from China, the Soviet Union, North Vietnam, North Korea, or Cuba, to foment and sustain guerrilla insurgency. External areas can also provide a sanctuary and escape route that severely limits the effectiveness of counterinsurgency operations. As a result, there is often a need for close coordination of planning, command, training, equipment, and logistics between the police and military forces in the less-developed countries, more particularly in Asia and Latin America, to facilitate effective joint operations against insurgency.

RELATIONSHIPS BETWEEN
FORCE AND DEVELOPMENT

Several relationships may arise between military force and economic development; in some cases, military and economic programs may hinder—and in others, facilitate—each other's tasks. If it is possible to identify the points of conflict and of complementarity, policies and programs can be developed that minimize the conflicts and take advantage of potential complementarities. The following discussion is concerned with some of the general relationships that are involved, and later chapters will take up specific aspects in more detail.

[20] See Chapter Five, pp. 106–107.

There are a number of important respects in which military and economic programs, both foreign aid and domestic programs, are likely to conflict with one another. So far as United States aid programs are concerned, increased appropriations for military aid may reduce the amount available for economic aid, and vice versa. The extent of this conflict depends both on the degree to which Congress regards economic and military aid as alternatives, and on the extent to which Congress and the Administration are concerned with keeping total government appropriations within some limit. Moreover, once appropriations have been made, the conflict between military and economic aid funds may continue if the legislation permits transfers between programs and purposes of the Foreign Assistance Act.

Similarly, domestic military programs in the less-developed countries may absorb scarce materials, equipment, and services that would otherwise be available for development programs or for programs to redistribute wealth and income. Perhaps even more important than the resources are the interest, attention, and effort of leaders and organizers who, to the extent they are concerned with military affairs, may be less concerned with development programs.

There are less direct ways in which the implementation of one set of programs may make the tasks of the other set more difficult. As noted earlier, the process of economic development may actually increase ·internal insecurity, at least in the short run. Typically, traditional societies have developed a variety of institutions for sharing the burdens and costs of birth, marriage, employment, and unemployment among the family, clan, or village. As economic development progresses, these stabilizing institutions may be weakened before effective substitutes have evolved. As a result, the burdens of adversity may impinge more directly on the individual. While economic conditions in the aggregate are improving, these burdens may become a more severe hardship for a large number of individuals who, as a consequence, provide ready recruits for organized subversion. Such circumstances, which may be typical even during periods of rapid economic development, can contribute to a heightened risk of internal insecurity and subversion. The result may be that the use of military and police forces becomes more difficult; put another way, the "output," in terms of internal security and stability, from a given military program may be reduced by virtue of economic development.

To get at another possible conflict between economic and military programs, we might ask the question: "What effect may increased rates of economic development in some of the less-developed countries have on the probability of external aggression and external support for internal subversion against them?" Although the argument is necessarily speculative, the probability of local aggression against a successfully developing country on the periphery of, say, China might increase as a result of that development.

Consider, for example, the effect of successful growth in India on the likelihood of Chinese military action or subversion in Ladakh, the Northeast Frontier, or in Sikkim or Bhutan; indeed, consider the effect of India's moderately successful growth between 1956 and 1961 on the motivation behind China's aggressive actions in October 1962. There are several reasons why development in India might increase the incentives for Chinese action: (1) A demonstration of "effective" growth under free institutions might have a sufficiently uncomfortable impact within China to raise the value to China's leaders of interfering with such growth; (2) Effective economic performance in India might cause China to attribute a lower probability to the prospective collapse of India's noncommunist political system without external aggression. If China views the value of aggression against India as the *difference* between what would result with and without the aggression, a reduced probability of internal collapse in India might raise that value to the Chinese; (3) More rapid growth in India might simply make it a more valuable asset for the communist system to absorb, and external aggression could be used to facilitate internal takeover by an Indian communist government. Within limits, weak performance may provide some insurance against attack by lowering the value of the prize.[21] However, since weakness may also reduce the costs of capturing it, the outcome is unclear.

Hence, effective economic growth in countries on the Chinese pe-

---

[21] It is worth noting that the considerations discussed in Chapter One that affect the value of particular countries to the United States may, in different degrees, affect their value to the Soviet Union, or to China, or to other communist countries.

riphery might actually increase the probability of Chinese aggression as a way of interfering with this growth. Of course, the interference might take different forms and be of varying intensity: border provocations intended to divert Indian resources from development to defense; a Chinese commitment in strength to take over a border region in Bhutan or Sikkim or in northern Laos; stepped-up support for indigenous guerrilla forces or for other "proxy" forces, for example, for the North Vietnamese in South Vietnam. Indeed, a case can be made in support of this view as an explanation for the intensification of guerrilla activities in South Vietnam after 1960. The marked economic and social improvements accomplished by the Diem regime from 1955 to 1960—dramatic by comparison with the economic stagnation in North Vietnam—raised the stake that the communist countries were willing to risk on efforts to disrupt the regime.

Granted these points of conflict between them, military and economic programs can also complement one another. One such complementarity arises from the fact that each program can confer spillover benefits on the other. Thus, economic development can raise the effectiveness of military programs by increasing the total resource base on which defense budgets can draw, by raising educational and literacy levels, and by adding to the stock of technological skills that the military can use. The public utilities and services ("infrastructure") that are expanded during economic growth may also enhance the mobility of military forces, and facilitate surveillance and intelligence activities by providing better transport and communications. Although economic development may create social stresses, strains, and potential dissidence, it may also provide a way of enlisting the energies and the loyalties of potential dissidents, and a means of eventually attracting actual dissidents away from guerrilla warfare.

Complementarities also operate in the reverse direction. The most powerful of these is both obvious and frequently neglected: Without security against internal and external aggression, ongoing production can be disrupted and economic development cannot make headway. Opportunities and motivations to invest, to acquire and apply improved technology, to maintain regular working habits, and to increase labor skills, depend on adequate security and on the expectation that it will be maintained. Consequently, military and paramilitary programs that deter external attack, control internal subversion, and improve law and order are essential for effective economic development programs.

Israel provides the most striking example of the contribution made to economic growth by programs that deter and control external attack. Vietnam provides two further examples of this relationship: the intimate connection between a moderate degree of internal security and rapid economic growth, during the period from 1955 to 1960; and that between internal insecurity and economic disruption in the period since 1961. As the Draper Committee observed in 1959:

> Without internal security and the general feeling of confidence engendered by adequate military force, there is little hope for any economic progress.[22]

There is a threshold beyond which further improvements in law, order, and security probably have no effect, or even a negative effect, on the productivity of economic programs. Most of the advanced countries, for example those in NATO, are beyond this security threshold. On the other hand, most of the underdeveloped countries on the Sino-Soviet periphery, and perhaps in Latin America and Africa, are probably well within it. It is worth pointing out that in countries operating below this threshold the military forces and capabilities that are needed to maintain security may frequently entail more than paramilitary, police, and other conventional internal security forces. Forces to close a border, or to seal a corridor that is an infiltration route, or to provide a capability for special operations inside adjacent communist areas, may involve costs and equipment greater than those that are usually associated with police functions.

Military programs can also contribute to economic development by providing a wider market for domestic production, including but not confined to military equipment. In some cases the stimulus provided by a reliable military demand may enable domestic producers to realize economies of large-scale output that permit a lowering of

---

[22] The President's Committee to Study the United States Military Assistance Program (The Draper Committee), *Composite Report*, Vol. 1, Washington, D. C., 1959, p. 149.

costs and prices, and result eventually in access to new *civilian* markets at home and abroad. Thus, in both Taiwan and Turkey this has begun to happen in the production of communications equipment, electrical equipment, hand tools, and automotive parts. Although other methods of stimulating demand may be preferable, where military forces and programs are needed for security reasons, the economic benefits that can be derived from military demand should not be overlooked.

Besides these side effects, military programs can produce output that is *directly* valuable to the civilian economy. For example, outlays on military programs can be used for building various infrastructures, for financing technical training programs, and for supporting engineering and construction battalions, all of which may have joint civil and military value. Such opportunities for joint production have an important bearing on improved programming of military aid and related programs, as will be discussed later. Moreover, the training in basic literacy and in habits of discipline and organization that military service affords may provide skills of high value to the civilian economy.

Typically, military tasks or missions can be performed in different ways. For example, in meeting or deterring external aggression, increased military effectiveness can be "bought" by providing larger indigenous forces; or, alternatively, by building an appropriate ground environment that will facilitate more rapid intervention of United States or allied forces. In some contingencies, one alternative may be preferable; in others, a different alternative. The *military* consequences of some equal-cost alternatives may be quite similar, although their economic side effects may be substantially different, as will be suggested in Chapter Seven, "Defense and Development." In such cases, where the primary criterion, relating to military effectiveness, yields approximately equivalent results for several programs, choice should be based on *secondary criteria* concerning economic and social side effects.

Finally, military threats and programs to meet them may elicit responses that will contribute to economic development in several ways. A sense of emergency and patriotism generated by the threat may raise savings rates; foreign aid for both military and economic programs may be increased; and bottlenecks that have hampered economic development under peacetime conditions may be broken. It is interesting to note in this connection that the Reserve Bank of India's report on the country's economic development during the fiscal year ending March 31, 1963, divided that period into two phases: the first before, and the second after, the Chinese invasion of India's northern borders in October 1962. Besides the enactment of higher taxes and measures to control gold hoarding and smuggling,

> . . . the second phase saw a better export performance, a large inflow of foreign aid, a distinct improvement in industrial production facilitated, among other things, by better utilization of capacity, efforts to eliminate bottlenecks and better cooperation from labor.[23]

Still, whatever stimulus to Indian development may have been provided by the Chinese aggression was confined to the short run. Subsequent events suggest that the initial impetus to decision making subsided rapidly, and that renewed competition for scarce resources between military and economic programs intensified India's economic difficulties.[24]

In general, the competitive effects between military and economic programs probably exceed the complementary effects, which is, after all, a basic reason for making a budgetary and analytical distinction between these categories of assistance in the first place. Nevertheless, the complementarities are of sufficient importance that policies and programs (which recognize, for example, the role of secondary economic and social criteria in choosing among alternative military programs) should be designed to take advantage of the opportunities they offer.[25] Indeed, in many of the less-developed countries the military establishment may be a relatively effective, if not the inevitable, institution for contributing to the civil as well as the military ingredients of nation building.

[23] Reserve Bank of India, *Indian News Digest*, Bombay, July 1, 1963, summarized in International Monetary Fund, *International Financial News Survey*, Washington, D. C., August 9, 1963, p. 1.
[24] For a discussion of India's problems in this and other fields, see George Rosen, *Democracy and Economic Change in India*, Berkeley and Los Angeles, University of California Press, 1966.
[25] For an example, see below pp. 132–140.

CHAPTER THREE

Insurgency and
Counterinsurgency

Since World War II, acute insurgency has occurred frequently in the less-developed areas. There has rarely been a year when at least one was not under way—in Greece, Burma, Malaya, the Philippines, Vietnam, Laos, the Congo, Algeria, Cuba, Yemen, or the Dominican Republic. In the next decade it is likely to be no less prevalent. While each insurgency is in some sense unique, most of them have shared many common features—tactics, violence, organization, and ideology. The common features make insurgency a legitimate subject for more general consideration, while the prominence and frequency of insurgency identify it as a major problem for United States policies and programs—past, present, and future—in the third world.

What are the sources and causes of insurgency? What concepts and doctrine can help in understanding it? What programs can be formulated to deter insurgency, and what types of programs are likely to control or suppress insurgency once it has gathered momentum? Both as practical and as intellectual problems, insurgency and counterinsurgency provide a meeting ground for the intricate cross-currents of the cold war: nationalism, revolutionary political change, economic and social development, and military and paramilitary strategy and tactics. The following discussion will try to relate the general themes

46

of Chapter Two to insurgency and counterinsurgency in the third world.

THE CENTRAL ROLE
OF "POPULAR SUPPORT"

The core of currently accepted doctrine about insurgency is that popular attitudes, loyalties, and support play a dominant role in the process by which insurgent movements get started, gain momentum, and erupt in "liberation wars." The doctrine is not usually so over-drawn as to assign the full burden of explanation to popular sympathy. International politics, external assistance, and military factors are also acknowledged to play a role. But these roles are subsidiary and permissive, according to the doctrine, and the primary, activating force behind insurgency movements lies in popular likes and dislikes, the erosion of mass support for established institutions, and the gaining of popular support and commitment by the insurgency. In the same manner, the doctrine contends that successful counterinsurgency programs require that support be won from the insurgents by the established government.

Certain key phrases reflect the mood of this doctrine: the familiar "fish in the sea" analogy; the view that insurgency and counterinsurgency are "political, social, and economic rather than military problems"; the claim that insurgency and counterinsurgency are "struggles for men's minds rather than for territory." These are the phrases and metaphors used by practitioners like Mao, Giap, and Guevara.[1] They are also the terms in which the problem is formulated by many analysts and commentators, such as Roger Hilsman, Walter Lippmann, Peter Paret, John Shy, and Bernard Fall.[2]

---

[1] For Mao, guerrilla warfare is a special case of the general proposition that "Weapons are an important factor in war, but not the decisive one; it is man and not material that counts," Mao Tse-Tung, *Selected Works*, Vol. II, p. 192, International Publishers, New York, 1954.

However, to keep the picture properly balanced, it is worth noting that Mao is also the originator of the aphorism that "political power grows out of the barrel of a gun," *ibid.*, p. 272.

[2] See, for example, Peter Paret and John W. Shy, "Guerrilla Warfare and U.S. Military Policy: A Study," in *The Guerrilla—and How to Fight Him*, T. N.

This thesis about popular support is usually tied in closely with the contention that economic and social programs can prevent the loss of popular sympathy for established institutions, or can win popular loyalty away from the insurgency. In this form, the prevailing doctrine is one of the principal themes pervading both policy pronouncements and journalistic reporting of insurgency. For example, the doctrine was clearly expressed by one of the senior officials in the Agency for International Development in congressional testimony on the Foreign Assistance Act:

> The [counterinsurgency] concept essentially rests on the assumption that this kind of war depends heavily upon the psychology of the peasant, his attitude toward his government, and toward his future. If we can quickly demonstrate to him the prospect of improvement in his livelihood, in his children's future, then he will not be vulnerable to the propaganda and terror of the insurgents.[3]

Along the same lines, a staff writer for the *Wall Street Journal* reported and endorsed this view of the war in Vietnam in the summer of 1964:

> Most American observers in South Vietnam say that if the U.S.-backed war against Communist insurgents is to make any progress, the Saigon regime must win the loyalty and confidence of the residents of the Vietnamese countryside. And the only way to achieve this goal, these Americans assert, is for the government to convince the 15 million citizens of South Vietnam that it can solve long-neglected social and economic problems and improve drab-substandard living conditions.[4]

Greene (ed.), New York, Frederick A. Praeger, Inc., 1962, pp. 39–43. Fall is more difficult to classify; sometimes he appears to take the view described in the text, and sometimes he appears to oppose it. See, for example, his *Street Without Joy*, Harrisburg, The Stackpole Co., 1963, pp. 353–356. For some notable exceptions to the views described in the text, see James E. Cross, *Conflict in the Shadows: The Nature and Politics of Guerrilla War*, New York, Doubleday and Co., 1963, especially pp. 31–39; and David Galula, *Counter-Insurgency Warfare*, New York, Frederick A. Praeger, Inc., 1964.

[3] *Foreign Assistance Act of 1964*, Hearings before the Committee on Foreign Affairs, House of Representatives, 88th Congress, 2nd Session, April 1964, p. 208.

[4] *Wall Street Journal*, June 15, 1964, p. 1.

Representing the views on Vietnam of at least part of the American scientific community, an editorial comment in the *Bulletin of the Atomic Scientists* recently observed that:

> [The war in Vietnam] is a guerrilla war, and the winning of such a war requires the allegiance, or at least the passive support, of the population. This has been conspicuously absent for the obvious reason that South Vietnam has not had and is not getting a government in contact with its people.[5]

The Honolulu Declaration by President Johnson and Premier Ky in February 1966 affirmed that: "The war for the hearts of the people is more than a military tactic. It is a moral principle. For this we shall strive as we fight to bring about a true social revolution."[6]

These quotations relect a style of thinking and a pattern of belief about insurgency and counterinsurgency problems that is as pervasive as it is untested. This new mythology implies a logic which, for the purpose of analysis, we shall put in the form of a syllogism:

(1) Insurgent movements require popular support in order to gain momentum, and guerrilla forces require popular support in order to conduct successful military operations. Similarly, acquiring popular support by the government is essential if counterguerrilla operations are to be successful. (For example, adherents typically claim that the growth of the Viet Cong after 1960 reflected increasing popular sympathy for the insurgency, and the alienation of popular support by Diem and his successors.)

(2) If popular support for the insurgents is to be neutralized, and if it is to be acquired by the counterinsurgents, the government must provide economic and social benefits to the rural areas in which the bulk of the population lives. (Thus, the alleged failure of Diem and his successors to alleviate socio-economic ills and injustices, and to provide effective programs for rural betterment, have been advanced as explanations for their inability to control and defeat the Viet Cong.)

[5] *Bulletin of the Atomic Scientists*, April 1965, p. 2.
[6] *Presidential Report*, Congressional Quarterly, February 11, 1966, p. 379.

(3) Therefore, socio-economic improvement programs, especially in rural areas, are essential for an effective counterinsurgency effort.[7]

The syllogism has undeniable appeal to those grounded in Western ideologies and values. It strikes a particularly responsive chord in the populist symbols and sentiments of American traditions. But it may be stronger on symbolism and sentiment than on realism. As a basis for describing the problem and for prescribing remedies, it probably involves significant inaccuracies in both the major and minor premises, hence in the inference drawn from them. This chapter will raise some questions about the logic behind the syllogism, and consider an alternative approach to the analysis of insurgency.

SOME QUESTIONS
ABOUT POPULAR SUPPORT

Consider the major premise (1). It can be argued that an opposite position is both logically and empirically tenable. *Given the characteristics of transitional societies in the less-developed countries*, an effective insurgency and guerrilla activity can grow and gather momentum among a population that is passive or even hostile to the movement. The growth of the Viet Cong and of the Pathet Lao probably occurred despite the opposition of a large majority of the people in both Vietnam and Laos. And embryonic insurgency in Thailand can wax in the future despite the indifference or hostility of most of the people toward the movement. By the same token, successful counterinsurgency programs can be conducted among a rural populace that is passive or even hostile, rather than loyal, to the government.

What an insurgent movement requires for successful and expand-

---

[7] After 1965 the war in Vietnam perhaps attained a level of violence beyond the point at which adherents of this doctrine would claim that it applies. At the same time, most adherents would be inclined to say that further escalation (in the form of expanded bombing of North Vietnam, and naval blockades along the coast) will not bring any significant improvement in the counterinsurgency effort in South Vietnam because it will not influence popular support. Rather than influencing the insurgency, escalation may simply turn that conflict into a different type of war.

ing operations is not popular support, in the sense of attitudes of identification and allegiance, but rather a supply of certain *inputs* (*e.g.*, food, recruits, information) at reasonable cost, interpreting "cost" to include expenditure of coercion as well as of money. These costs may be "reasonable" *without* popular sympathy for the insurgents, and, conversely, the costs may be considerably augmented without any increase in allegiance to the government. This is the crux of the alternative approach that will be developed later. The point to make here is simply that the usual emphasis on popular support may be misleading. Resources that the insurgents need from rural areas may continue to be available and at reasonable or perhaps even reduced cost, notwithstanding increased popular support for the government. Conversely, these resource flows may be interdicted, or made more costly to the insurgency without any increase in popular support for the government. In the actual environment of transitional societies, once an insurgent movement has attained some modest level of organization and activity, increases in popular support for the government are more likely to be the result than the cause of effective counterinsurgent action by the government. Clausewitz' assertion that "public opinion ultimately depends on great victories" is not without significance in the counterinsurgency context.

Now consider the minor premise (2), concerning the relationship between popular support and socio-economic improvement programs. Does social and economic development increase popular support, or does it create antagonism (because of the inevitable insufficiency of the improvement with respect to an aspiration level which may be raised by the improvement programs themselves)? Does development impede extremist movements, or does it facilitate them by promoting social instability and dislocation? Does development foster a more competitive, open society, or does it instead require a centralization of power and control that conflicts with liberal institutions, at least in the short run? As already noted in Chapter Two, these basic questions have been extensively studied, debated, and subjected to preliminary empirical tests, without decisive results.[8] Both questions and

---

[8] In addition to the references cited in footnote 4 of chapter two, see Mancur Olson, Jr., "Rapid Growth as a Destabilizing Force," *Journal of Economic*

answers involve phenomena that are complex and imperfectly understood. Still, at most, it must be said that there is no conclusive evidence to sustain the view that economic and social improvement programs have a predictable and positive effect on popular support.

But from the standpoint of insurgency and counterinsurgency, there is a more important point than the extent to which social and economic improvement programs influence popular support. Even if such programs do increase popular support, *there may be no effect, or a perverse effect, on the cost and availability of inputs that the insurgents require for their operations.* As will be discussed later, the effects are likely to be sensitive to the criteria used in determining the types of economic projects that are undertaken, and where they are located. Nevertheless, for certain types of programs, it is entirely possible that the effects may be perverse. The supply of what the insurgents need from the villages may expand and its cost may decline, *notwithstanding increased popular support for the government.*

The reason for this apparent paradox is not hard to find. Economic and social development programs, while they may affect the preferences of the populace as between government and insurgents, will expand the disposable resources with which the populace can supply the insurgency. Even if the villager's allegiance to the government is increased, the fact that he commands additional resources as a result of economic improvement will enable him to use more of these resources to "buy" his security (protection) from the insurgent forces. Economic and social development programs in an insurgent environment thus have a sure effect on *income,* as well as a possible effect on preferences. The effect on preferences may increase the villager's liking for the government, but the income effect will certainly increase the resources available to him for reaching an accommodation with the insurgents on terms that make him feel he is improving his chances of survival. The existence of hostility by the rural populace toward the insurgents does not rule out an arrangement between

History, December 1963; James R. Schlesinger, *The Political Economy of National Security,* New York, Frederick A. Praeger, Inc., 1960, pp. 224–227; Wolf, *Foreign Aid, op. cit.,* Chapters 8 and 9; and below, Chapter Five, "Military Programs and Political Effects."

them in which both can benefit as a result of economic and social improvement projects undertaken by the central government.

Our conclusion thus contrasts sharply with the conclusion of the conventional syllogism. Improvement programs may or may not increase popular support for the government. But whether or not there is an improvement in popular support, the effect is more likely to facilitate the growth of the insurgent movement, and to increase the effectiveness of its guerrilla operations, than to impede it. Rural improvement programs, in order to be of any benefit as an adjunct of counterinsurgency efforts, must attempt to exact *something in return* for whatever benefits are provided. The allocation of resources for such programs must be part of a bargaining operation in which the government's improvement projects are exchanged for restrictions that limit the availability of resources that the insurgency can draw from rural areas.

The objective of winning popular allegiance to a government that is combating an insurgent movement, though a desirable goal, is probably too broad and too ambitious to serve as a conceptual framework for counterinsurgency programs. It is too broad because it cannot discriminate between government actions that hinder and those that help insurgent operations; it is too ambitious because it is beyond the capacity of an overburdened and embattled government to overcome in short order the antigovernmental attitudes that are deeply engrained in transitional societies. In such societies, the government is traditionally viewed as an opponent rather than a friend: as the tax collector, conscripter, warmaker, buyer of output (at low prices)—as "they," not "us." (According to an old Burmese proverb, "The four things which cannot be trusted are thieves, the boughs of trees, women, and rulers.")

To develop modern societies, it is of course necessary to change these attitudes, but it is unrealistic to expect that they will be drastically modified in five or twenty-five years. The attitudes are too deeply engrained, and the animosities and rigidities on which they are based are too numerous and deep-seated to be eradicated quickly. Increasing popular loyalty for the government by changing these attitudes is more likely to be a consequence than a cause of successful counterinsurgency. The operational problem, therefore, is how to increase the effectiveness of counterinsurgency efforts directly; how to influence behavior and action in the short run so that attitudes and loyalties can be altered in the long run.

AN ALTERNATIVE APPROACH

As suggested earlier, transitional societies are inherently vulnerable to insurgency. Cleavages and antagonisms are endemic and pervasive: between landlords and tenants; between urban and rural areas; among ethnic, racial, religious, and linguistic groups. Inequities in the distribution of wealth, income, education, and opportunity are chronic, widespread, and often painful. Resentment against privilege and status enjoyed by foreigners and domestic elites is often acute or easily inflamed. Such patterns of bitterness and resentment are as much a part of the realities of transitional societies as are low income levels. To change these patterns requires far-reaching changes in social, political, and economic structure. If such changes come about under nonauthoritarian auspices, they are likely to result only after a generation or more. If they come about under communist or other equally severe auspices, they may be quicker, but they will bring with them new and harsher torments.

The legacy of discontent and grievance that characterizes the less-developed countries puts pressure on governmental and other institutions whose capabilities for dealing with the underlying causes are extremely limited. Even with good leadership and the best use of these limited capabilities, a successful attack on the causes will take time and accomplishments will be spotty. Innumerable evils and grievances are bound to persist, and insurgent movements will probably be able to exploit them, by combining a modest investment of ingenuity, organization, and external support with the lure of acquiring power. Thus, there will remain a high probability that an adequate number of people can be found who are willing to support and participate in an insurgent movement. The promise of gain does not have to be much to attract those with little to lose.

Under these circumstances, the most that governments may be able to do in a decade or two is to mitigate some of the more egregious sources of discontent. Some social injustices may be reduced, and economic development may be started. But, inevitably, a large residue of discontent and grievance will remain. To say that transitional societies are vulnerable to insurgency is to state a truism.

In this context, an approach to counterinsurgency that focuses on "winning popular support" has little chance of success. There are too many obstacles to surmount, and too many reasons why whatever support is won is likely to be lukewarm and easily alienated. A more modest approach may be at once more realistic and more useful.

The alternative approach to be explored here starts from the observation that insurgent movements should be viewed as operating systems or organizations, requiring certain *inputs*, from either local or foreign sources, which are converted into the *outputs* characterizing the active insurgency. In general, insurgency requires inputs of recruits, information, shelter, and food that usually are obtained from the local environment; and cadres, publicity, materiel, and funds that often can be provided from external sources. To obtain the necessary inputs from the local environment, the insurgency relies on various coercive as well as persuasive techniques. Coercion may take many forms: kidnaping, assassination, torture, threats, forcible tax collection, destruction or confiscation of property, crop or land seizure (especially in the case of unpopular landowners). But needed inputs may also be obtained by persuasion and inducements rather than by coercion: propaganda and indoctrination, money payments, village-aid projects, technical education and training, and by opportunities for action, promotion, and affiliation with a worthy cause. Coercion may be a relatively more efficient means of obtaining compliance (or eliminating opposition) from those who initially have something appreciable to lose in income, wealth, or position. On the other hand, inducements may be the more efficient means of eliciting the behavior that is wanted from those who have little to lose, and who therefore tend to magnify any gains by comparison. Perhaps this is why the Viet Cong have generally used coercion against village leaders and the well-to-do, and inducements in obtaining needed inputs from the ordinary villagers.

In any event, the inputs that are obtained through this combination of inducement and coercion are converted into outputs by the insurgent organization. A combination of inducements (recognition, reward, promotion) and coercion (criticism, isolation, demotion, and physical punishment) is used again in the conversion process. As with any organization, the insurgency relies on intelligence, personnel, financial, logistics, and communications functions or branches to manage the conversion of inputs into outputs. When an insurgency is beginning as a small-scale operation, these functions will be fused; as it grows and gathers momentum, they are apt to become separate and specialized.

The outputs of the insurgent system include acts of sabotage, terror, public demonstrations, small-scale attacks, and eventually larger attacks and mobile warfare directed against the civil instrumentalities of government (e.g., village, district, and provincial functionaries; public services) and against the government's military and paramilitary forces.

Our alternative approach divides the problem of counterinsurgency into two parts. One part of the problem is to raise the cost and reduce the availability of the inputs that the insurgency requires. The second part is to curtail the outputs of the system by interfering with the process by which inputs are converted into outputs, and by directly blocking or destroying the outputs. Military measures are the principal means of directly curtailing the system's outputs. Economic, social, and political programs, as well as military efforts, are needed to impede the supply of inputs to the system, as well as their conversion into outputs.

Concerning the military, output-oriented programs, one point appears clear from counterinsurgency experience in Malaya, the Philippines, and Algeria. The military programs needed to curtail active insurgency require large quantities of manpower; they are labor-intensive rather than capital-intensive programs. The large numbers are reflected by the familiar ratio of 10 counterinsurgents to 1 insurgent, a ratio that is often cited although usually without too clear a picture of what should be included in either numerator or denominator.[9]

In designing the nonmilitary, input-oriented measures, explicit consideration should be given to whether and how a particular activity is likely to impede the flow of inputs to the insurgents. Policies and projects that might be normally desirable may be quite inappropriate in the presence of an insurgency because they would not increase the insurgents' costs of obtaining their needed inputs. Indeed, policies that would increase rural income by raising food prices, or projects that would increase agricultural productivity through distribution of fertilizer or livestock, may be of negative value during an insurgency. As noted earlier, such projects and programs may actually facilitate guerrilla operations by increasing the availability of inputs that the insurgents need.

IMPLICATIONS OF
THE ALTERNATIVE APPROACH

What difference would such an approach make? It may be worthwhile to consider the differences at two levels: the first, relating to our general attitude toward the governments we collaborate with in counterinsurgency programs; the second, relating to specific operational suggestions for dealing with insurgency problems.

Because Americans typically start from the previously described "popular-support" view, we frequently feel uncomfortable collaborating with established governments against insurgent movements. Notwithstanding our awareness of the realities of communist subversion and the techniques of "liberation war," the populist tradition in American history disposes us to identify with the insurgent ethos. The initial role of a Castro evokes more sympathy among Americans than that of a Batista. Castro, struggling in the Sierra Maestra, could be easily

[9] A number of interesting questions, that will not be discussed here, arise in connection with these military programs: for example, the types of weaponry and forces; the efficient mix between military and paramilitary units; and trade-offs between manpower and equipment, and between helicopters and fixed-wing aircraft, in the conduct of these programs.

seen as a popular, Jacksonian crusader for the common man and against the entrenched interests; Batista fitted equally well the role of the ruthless, exploitative tyrant. That there was reality as well as appearance in this role-casting is not the point. The point is that the emotional reaction of Americans to insurgencies frequently interferes with a realistic assessment of alternatives, and inclines us instead toward a carping righteousness in our relations with the beleagured government we are ostensibly supporting.

Moreover, when we find that our initial effort to support an established government in quelling an insurgency turns out less than a smashing success, our disposition to accept and to advocate the popular-support view provides a way for us to extenuate our poor showing. Casting the established government in the role of tyrant, vested interest, and exploiter deflects the blame for ineffectual performance from our own bad advice and assistance, and places it instead on the misconduct of the established government. If the effort founders, the explanation *must* be the villainy of our ally, rather than our own errors or the ingenuity and energy of the adversaries. Something of this general mood became increasingly influential in molding our relationships with Diem and his regime in Vietnam in late 1962 and 1963.

The effect of such a change in attitude is that we become a hostile and captious critic of the established regime, which begins to regard us as an adversary rather than a collaborator. In the process, we may lose whatever influence and leverage we might otherwise have had to bring about modest but important improvements in policies and programs. When we expend effort and exhaust good will in a querulous homily about the need to gain mass popular support, we may miss opportunities to bring about piecemeal and gradual improvements in counterinsurgency programs.

It is by no means far-fetched to imagine that this same sequence might ensue in our efforts to improve and extend counterinsurgency programs in Thailand or elsewhere in the future. We may begin with an awareness that the insurgency movement is in part traceable to communist organization and resources, as well as to internal sources of grievance and discontent. But as we find that the problem persists or even grows worse, we may be increasingly disposed to cast the established regime in the familiar role of a villain, whose inability to acquire popular support among the people is evidenced by the persistence of insurgency.

This is *not* to deny that many of the governments that we have to deal with do in fact possess some of these evil characteristics. But, to repeat, the point is that our disposition to accept the popular-support view of the problem often makes us prone to look for overly broad and ambitious "social-transformation" solutions, and to overlook the more modest, realistic, and sometimes distasteful measures that may improve the situation step by step.

What specific operational suggestions might be inferred from the alternative approach we have been exploring? Clearly, to translate this approach into operationally useful countermeasures requires a detailed understanding of how the particular insurgent system actually operates. Where does it get its inputs? In what quantities and at what costs? How are inputs converted into outputs? Who receives information and who evaluates it? Who exercises command over personnel, equipment, funds, and logistics? Where do (or might) frictions, cleavages, ambiguities, and misunderstandings arise in the insurgency's hierarchy, and how might they be abetted?

Countering an ongoing insurgency requires a detailed understanding of how the organization functions in specific contexts. However, the following paragraphs illustrate the alternative approach in general terms, suggesting several types of countermeasures that might be useful, some of them based on the experience and methods used by President Magsaysay in waging effective counterinsurgency against the Hukbalahap in the Philippines in the early 1950's. The unifying theme of these measures is that they are primarily directed toward influencing *behavior*, rather than attitudes, by raising the costs and reducing the availability of inputs needed by the insurgency movement.

FOOD SUPPLIES

Looking at the specific problem of reducing the availability of food to feed the insurgency, several measures are worth considering. Civil or military units of the established government might try to buy up rural food supplies in order to deny them to the insurgents. Pre-emptive buying of this sort clearly would entail a risk: The rural sup-plier of food would get money in return, and this might simply have the effect of increasing the disposable income which the insurgents could then tax. However, the food might be acquired through barter transactions using other consumer goods, such as textiles or tobacco, which are valuable to the rural population as consumers but are of relatively little value to the insurgents. In this way it might be possi-ble to pre-empt food supplies without providing the insurgents with additional income to use in buying food on the open market. A pre-emptive buying program, using barter as payment, might seriously complicate the logistics of insurgent operations.

RECRUITMENT AND DEFECTION

An insurgent organization typically draws its recruits from the locale in which it operates. The local recruits are attracted for various rea-sons: the worthy causes associated with the insurgent movement, the desire to redress social injustices, the adventure associated with guer-rilla activity, and the possibility of personal advancement—in contrast to the tedium and stagnation of village life. Threats and coercion are used selectively, but severely, to make these attractions effective; in general, the greater the attractions, the less coercion must be ex-pended by the insurgents to obtain needed recruits.

A number of measures by the counterinsurgency might make re-cruitment less attractive, and, by influencing the hypothetical men at the margin, might reduce the supply of recruits, cause the insurgency to expend more coercion, and thereby complicate and obstruct in-surgent operations. Some of these measures involve improving the supply of information to the government so that guerrilla units can be more effectively harassed, and hence recruitment becomes less at-tractive. These measures will be discussed later. Other measures may operate on recruitment (and defection) without necessarily affecting informational inputs.

For example, the supply of recruits might be impeded by a judi-cious use of a device Magsaysay employed in the Philippines to motivate government forces to kill Huks: a promotion and a personal letter of praise to the effective government units from the president himself. Clearly, the dangers of a miscarriage of this system can be substantial. Used by a Batista, such an effort might yield results quite different from those achieved by Magsaysay. Nevertheless, some method of providing rewards for effective military action against insurgents can make a useful contribution both to motivating successful actions by government forces, and to making the prospect of guerrilla service less attractive to prospective recruits.

Another measure that was used effectively in the Philippines was the offer of amnesty to defecting Huks. Under the EDCOR program, they were resettled in Mindanao under terms that compared favorably with economic conditions prevailing in central Luzon: land, fertilizer, agricultural implements, and working capital were part of the package. Of course, the inducements might be made *too* attractive: villagers might join the insurgents in order to realize the benefits of subsequent defection, as reportedly occurred in Kenya during the Mau Mau uprising. However, the dilemma may be more apparent than real. The problem is how to make the life of a guerrilla look unattractive so that recruitment will be hindered, while at the same time making defection appear more attractive than the life of an insurgent so that those who do join are seriously tempted to defect. Amnesty and resettlement programs can probably be developed within a fairly wide range *without* augmenting the supply of recruits to the insurgent movement. In Vietnam, for example, the Chieu Hoi program (whose primary aim is the motivation and rehabilitation of defectors) surely operates so far within this range that it could improve its offerings substantially without running any risk of stimulating recruits to *join* the Viet Cong.

To take another example, the life of an insurgent might be made less appealing if the insurgents had fewer weapons to pass out to recruits. At the start of his counterinsurgency effort in the Philippines, Magsaysay offered a reward of 75 pesos ($38) for each serviceable unlicensed weapon returned to the government, *and no questions asked*. Buying up weapons, without inflicting any penalty on the person bringing them in, could reduce the fire power available to the insurgents, and thus make the life of a guerrilla less attractive. Again, there would be a risk: Government units might simply contrive to "lose" their weapons more frequently. However, this risk could be minimized by a system of reward or promotions for government troops that retain their weapons in combat, and of penalties for those that lose their weapons under noncombat conditions.

INFORMATION

Effective counterinsurgency requires both improvement in the supply of information to the government, and interference with the supply of information to the insurgents. To some extent the two efforts may be complementary. If incentives to provide information to the government are made stronger, the man at the margin may be induced to engage in this behavior rather than that of furnishing intelligence to the insurgents.

To the extent that the two efforts are independent of each other, the problem is more difficult. It is then easier to think of ways by which the supply of information to the government can be increased (and it is on these that the following comments will concentrate) than to think of ways by which the supply of information to the insurgents can be choked off. The one permits greater use of the carrot; the other invokes the stick and is a nastier route to travel. If the supply of information to the insurgents is to be reduced, those who have been identified as informers on government forces and units must be treated with severity. This, of course, is easier to say quickly than to do wisely; it runs the risk of excessive, misdirected, and counterproductive cruelty by government forces. Nevertheless, the point is important to recognize. As long as a fundamental asymmetry prevails in which information given to the government carries with it a high probability of quick and ruthless reprisal by the insurgents, while information given to the insurgents carries a negligible risk, the supply of intelligence is likely to be more abundant to the insurgents than to the government.

As to measures for increasing the supply of information to the government, the Philippine experience again is instructive. President Magsaysay instituted as one of his earliest counterinsurgency measures a system of substantial rewards for information leading to the capture of Huks: 500 pesos ($250) for enlisted men and 5000 pesos ($2500) for top leaders like Taruc, Lava, and Alejandrino (500 pesos was more than two and one half times the annual per capita income then prevailing in the Philippines).

The British, in suppressing the communist rebellion in Malaya, between 1948 and 1957 also made extensive use of direct payments to acquire information about communist guerrillas and officers. Prices were high for accurate information about the operations and personnel of the guerrilla organization, and payment was made rapidly. For example, it was not unusual for a Tamil rubber tapper to receive $25,000 if he provided reliable information concerning the whereabouts of four or five communist guerrillas and a district committee member.

If such an incentive system were at all effective in uncovering really useful information, the cost would be low. In Vietnam, for example, one might ask: "What is the 'price' of a Viet Cong?" If useful information could be obtained for $300 or more per head, the results could be quite dramatic at small cost. With a total force between 200,000 and 250,000, only a fraction of the Viet Cong would have to be located to create a seriously demoralizing effect on the insurgency's recruitment program. (And what, incidentally, would be the price at which the leaders of the Communist Committee for South Vietnam, or the National Front for the Liberation of South Vietnam, such as Nguyen Huu Tho, could be located? It might well be less than the price that Magsaysay paid for locating top Huk leaders in the Philippines.)[10]

Certainly, an incentive program of this sort places heavy burdens on the intelligence system of the established government to screen misinformation and to keep the effort from going amiss. Among other precautions, a careful system of prisoner interrogation, combined with a disciplined effort to be skeptical about the information received, would be advisable. Finally, as a vital part of these measures to im-

---

[10] Offering high prices might also expand information concerning the location of small arms and ammunition factories, which, at some stage of the insurgent movement, typically are set up in the area of operations. Here the dangers of misinformation and of a miscarriage of the effort are less than where the information concerns particular insurgents, whose identity may be more subject to question.

prove the supply of information to the government and to reduce the flow to the insurgents, it is essential to provide protection for the individuals or villages that furnish useful information on the location and operation of the insurgents. Otherwise the intended incentives will turn out to be unintended disincentives.

EXTERNAL INPUTS AND THE NEED TO CLOSE CONTIGUOUS BORDERS

As noted earlier, some of the inputs (cadres, money, and some types of materiel) that are important for the functioning of an insurgent system are frequently provided from abroad. The quantities are usually small in numbers or in tonnage, although their importance may be considerable. Where these inputs can be provided to the insurgency from a contiguous border area, the logistics of external support becomes relatively simple and its interdiction becomes difficult.

Although locally obtained inputs are of major importance to an insurgency movement, interdicting logistic support from contiguous border areas is necessary if a counterinsurgency effort is to succeed. In all cases where counterinsurgency efforts have been effective, there was either no contiguous land border (as in the Philippines) or the border was substantially closed off (as in Malaya and Greece). Insurgent movements may succeed in areas (Cuba) that lack a contiguous land border, but they are much more apt to win in areas (Viet Nam, Laos, and conceivably Thailand) where a contiguous border region provides an easy source of logistic support.

Of course, there is a substantial operational problem in closing a long contiguous border, particularly when the logistic support is modest in scale and irregular in timing. To coerce the external source of support by inflicting countervailing military or economic penalties on it (for example, the American bombing raids in North Vietnam) may be more efficient than manning a six- or seven-hundred mile border twenty-four hours a day. But bombing as a means of inflicting such penalties may encounter some operational difficulties as well as political problems that limit its scale and effectiveness. One difficulty is that the logistic support may be turned off and on much more readily than the bombing attacks.

However, there may be other ways of coercing communist sources of external support that are less subject to the political and other limitations of aerial bombardment. Communist countries, which typically operate through a network of extensive and rigid controls, may be especially vulnerable to measures that impede and undermine these controls. For example, one type of mischief to raise the cost of external support for insurgency might lie in introducing into the country of origin (for example, North Vietnam) counterfeit money, ration cards, and identity cards, as well as newspapers and leaflets containing various rumors, or hints of conspiracy by some officials against others. The rigidities of communist control systems may make them more vulnerable to such interference than are less tightly controlled, more flexible societies. Societies that are relatively open are less vulnerable to such measures for two reasons: They usually are less dependent than regimented societies on a wide range of tangible control devices, such as ration cards, identity cards, licenses, and official news media; and they are characterized by such a high level of "noise" in the form of rumors, false information, and conflicting views, under *normal* circumstances, that increments to the noise level are likely to be less bothersome and more easily absorbed than in communist societies.[11]

These suggestions have all related to particular inputs and sources of inputs that an insurgency system requires, and to possible measures for raising the costs of obtaining them or reducing their availability. In addition to the specific measures, there are two broad instruments which have a wider relevance in the design and implementation of counterinsurgency programs. The first concerns the discipline of government military and paramilitary forces; the second concerns the allocation of social and economic improvement programs as adjuncts of the counterinsurgency effort.

MILITARY DISCIPLINE

One of the more crippling impediments to effective counterinsurgency programs often lies in the wanton abuse of power by the government's

---

[11] I am indebted to Albert Wohlstetter for helping to clarify and elaborate this point.

military and paramilitary forces. The result of such abuses is not simply a weakening of support for and confidence in the government. The more serious reason that infractions of military discipline are counterproductive is that they are arbitrary and randomized. Hence, it becomes impossible for the populace to infer anything about the relationship between the harsh conduct of the government forces and their own *behavior*. Confiscation of chickens, razing of houses, or destruction of villages have a place in counterinsurgency efforts, but only if they are done for a strong reason: namely, to penalize those who have assisted the insurgents. If the reason for the penalty is not sufficient, explicit, and known to the people, exaction of penalties is likely to harm rather than help the counterinsurgency effort.

Military discipline must be tightened and brought under firm control so that whatever harshness is meted out by government forces is unambiguously recognizable as deliberately imposed because of behavior by the population that contributes to the insurgent movement. On the other hand, protection and benefits must be provided for individuals and villages whose actions assist the counterinsurgency effort. Military discipline must be strengthened not just to avoid capricious and unnecessary additions to the already large inventory of grievance and discontent; discipline must be strengthened mainly to amplify the signals that the government is trying to convey to the people concerning the kind of behavior that it wishes to promote and the kind that it wishes to discourage.

The progress of an insurgency movement increases the likelihood of misbehavior by government military forces; it is a frustration reaction that in turn strengthens the insurgency itself. To meet this problem in the Philippines, Magsaysay instituted a military Complaint Office with striking results. The victim of any abuse by the military was urged to report the incident. Following the report, an airplane from the Complaint Office arrived at the scene of the incident, and an investigation was held within two hours of receipt of the complaint. Rapid and effective action followed, combined with severe penalties against the offenders. The aim was not only to remove one of the more pressing and obvious sources of injustice and hostility, but also to reduce the "noise" interfering with the government's communication with the populace.

ECONOMIC AND SOCIAL IMPROVEMENT PROGRAMS

In setting up economic and social improvement programs, the crucial point is to connect such programs with the kind of population behavior the government wants to promote. Whether a program involves livestock, fertilizer, windmills, seeds, farm-to-market roads, or education, the choice and location of projects should reflect the principle of rewarding the villages that cooperate with the government and that withhold or limit the provision of tangible support for the insurgents. If incentives for cooperation are to be strengthened, it is also fundamental that economic and social improvement programs be combined with military protection of the cooperating rural areas.

There is another way in which social and economic improvement programs can influence the availability of inputs needed by the insurgents. One reason why it is difficult to restrict these inputs is that their sources are usually numerous and dispersed. Less-developed countries are usually "plural" economic and social entities in the sense that they contain many units that are functionally and technologically, as well as physically, remote from one another. Villages, districts, towns, provinces, and urban centers operate in imperfect contact, and often in isolation, from one another and particularly from the capital city and the institutions of the central government concentrated there. Thus, flows of commodities, information, and people from place to place are extremely limited.

Because the links and contacts among these enclaves, and between them and the center, are so meager, the government's ability to maintain surveillance and to establish control over the flow of inputs to an insurgency is accordingly limited. Under these circumstances, an important consideration when choosing economic and social improvement projects is the extent to which they will provide instruments for restricting the flow of inputs to the guerrillas. From this standpoint, projects that provide schools, dispensaries, roads, and other social services may be more effective than would economically more productive projects in, for example, agricultural development. Preferred projects, perhaps including civic-action projects by the military, are those that strengthen or expand the instruments available to the government for obtaining information and controlling insurgent logistics.

The two approaches to choosing economic and social projects differ, but they should often be mutually reinforcing. In one case, choice is based on providing rewards for the kind of behavior the government is trying to promote and, by withholding benefits and projects, on providing penalties for the kind of behavior it is trying to discourage. In the second case, choice is based on the extent to which particular projects in specific locations can forge the links that increase the government's ability to restrict the flow of inputs to the insurgency.

CONCLUSION

The difference between the usual emphasis on popular support, and the approach discussed here, is admittedly only a difference of degree. But degrees are often important, and at least two degrees of difference should be repeated in conclusion. At a broad, conceptual level, the main concern of counterinsurgency efforts should be to influence the behavior of the population rather than their loyalties and attitudes. Altering loyalties and attitudes is a long-run goal, to be achieved only gradually and with difficulty. It can be dramatically encouraged by the charismatic appeal of a Magsaysay, as an individual and a personality. But charismatic leadership is not a commodity that can be easily produced.[12] However, even without this rare attribute, improvements can be made. The leadership of countries in which insurgent movements appear can do much to influence the behavior and actions of the populace in ways that will make the operation of the insurgency substantially more difficult, and will facilitate counterinsurgency programs.

At the operational level, the main thrust of the approach we have

[12] Although it can be helped along in a number of ways. For some indications, see Jose V. Abueva, "Bridging the Gap Between the Elite and the People in the Philippines," in Geiger and Solomon (eds.), *Motivations and Methods in Development and Foreign Aid*, Washington, D. C., 1964, and Carlos P. Romulo and Marvin M. Gray, *The Magsaysay Story*, Toronto, Longmans, 1956.

been describing is to focus attention on the difficulties (or opportunities) that would be created for the insurgency by implementation of a proposed program or measure. The issue may concern fertilizer distribution or windmill construction, civic-action programs or military patrols; or it may be a matter of economic and social programs, intelligence-gathering programs, or military operations. But in all cases, the primary consideration should be whether the proposed measure is likely to increase the cost and difficulties of insurgent operations and help to disrupt the insurgent organization, rather than whether it wins popular loyalty and support, or whether it contributes to a more productive, efficient, or equitable use of resources.

Perhaps one major effect of the alternative approach may be to modify the attitudes with which *counter*insurgency efforts are viewed in the United States. Insurgency may be recognized *not* as an inscrutable and unmanageable force grounded in the mystique of a popular movement, but as a coherent system whose structure, calculations, and operations need to be understood if it is to be effectively countered.

CHAPTER
FOUR

The Uses and Limitations
of Nuclear Deterrence

Insurgency is probably the most likely type of politico-military threat
in the third world, and surely one of the most complex and challeng-
ing problems facing United States policies and programs. However,
the escalation of insurgent warfare can bring higher levels of violence
to the third world, as it did in Vietnam, and more directly in Korea in
1950, and, nearly, in Cuba in 1962. When we move from insurgency
to the higher rungs on the escalation ladder,[1] a question arises as to
the role and relevance of nuclear deterrence. Nothwithstanding the
United States-Soviet confrontation in the Cuban missile crisis, the
question bears largely on conflicts or potential conflicts in Asia. Consequently, the following discussion will be principally concerned with
that region.

[1] The "ladder" analogy is Herman Kahn's. See his *On Escalation: Scenarios and Metaphors*, Frederick A. Praeger, Inc., New York, 1965. Although suggestive, the analogy is imperfect for a number of reasons. When one climbs a ladder, all the rungs are visible and fixed throughout the climb. The forty-four rungs on Kahn's escalation ladder are neither fixed nor fully visible throughout the escalation process. Moreover, usually the only opposing force in ascending a ladder is gravity. The role of an intelligent adversary, who may oppose or seek to profit from the ascent, makes escalation very different from climbing.

TWO CONTRASTING VIEWS

There are two polar positions that are tacitly or explicitly held on this subject. At one extreme is the "broad-deterrent view," a position that used to be held more actively in some quarters, particularly in parts of the United States military establishment, than it currently is. According to the broad-deterrent view, the primary military threat in Asia is posed by Communist China, acting alone or through its proxies in North Vietnam and North Korea. This threat can be effectively deterred by a declaratory policy that focuses on the controlled use of nuclear weapons against targets in China, or in the proxy countries, at the upper limits of an escalation process that would first employ conventional weapons inside or outside the area of initial conflict, but would move rapidly to nuclear weapons if the precipitating aggression did not cease. The broad-deterrent view recognizes that the threat can —indeed, is likely to—take many forms besides large-scale, overt aggression. But it presumes that the underlying stimulus, support, and control of the aggression remain the responsibility of China or of its proxies. In Vietnam, therefore, pressure might be successfully applied on Tho (the putative political leader of the Viet Cong) by threatening and, if need be, hitting targets that are of value to Ho, or Mao. Hence, it is possible to use graduated *non*nuclear pressure, and, if this is not effective, nuclear weapons against the responsible parties themselves, thereby providing a potentially effective deterrent to lesser forms of provocation, as well.

At the opposite extreme is the "narrow-deterrent view," according to which nuclear weapons will probably not be effective or applicable in the kinds of contingencies that are likely to arise in Asia. (We will pass over the question of whether the ineffectiveness of nuclear deterrence in the contingencies that are *likely* to arise is itself an indication of the effectiveness of deterrence in rendering *unlikely* certain other contingencies.) According to this view, which has been held in many American and British quarters and is frequently expressed in France, the threat to use nuclear weapons in Asia is incredible because they would be ineffective; they would be ineffective because of the character of the Asian political environment, and also because of the nature of the conflicts that are generated by social, political, and economic changes in the area.

For reasons that include the World War II use of atomic weapons against Nagasaki and Hiroshima, it is argued that the Asian political environment will make the use of nuclear weapons inappropriate. The political costs that would be associated with their use would exceed whatever military gains might be obtained. Furthermore, the types of conflict that are bound to arise in Asia are too small, too ambiguous, and too deeply embedded in complex processes of social change, to give the use of nuclear weapons any plausibility. Other options (including withdrawal, perhaps) will always be more attractive than using nuclear weapons, so the threat of use is academic. Finally, according to the narrow-deterrent view, the major national interests of the nuclear powers are not so directly involved in Asia as they are in the defense of their own homeland. Hence, as De Gaulle has expressed it, it must be assumed that the nuclear powers will not "wish to assume the enormous risk of a general war," which a first use of nuclear weapons would entail in Asia as well as in Europe. (The reasoning here is analogous to and, in one sense, stronger than the argument that is sometimes made about the ineffectuality of the American deterrent in the European context, where American interests are more deeply involved than in Asia. However, the essential difference between the two contexts, which the quotation ignores, is the different *adversary* and the differing power that it possesses—a point we will return to later.)

The crucial distinction between the broad-deterrent and the narrow-deterrent views can be reduced to the question of the *threshold* of stimulus, provocation, or violence at which a United States nuclear response might be effective, and hence sufficiently credible to be a useful and reliable deterrent. That question, in turn, conceals a number of complex issues in Asia no less than in Europe. Would the use of nuclear weapons be militarily effective? (Are there targets within the initial area of conflict that can be more effectively destroyed with nuclear weapons than with other means, without inflicting more significant damage on friend than on foe? If not, then is geographic escalation with nuclear weapons against targets outside the tactical area likely to be more effective than conventional weapons in relieving the military threat? Is there a risk that use of nuclear weapons will involve the Soviet Union in further escalation moves?) Are the political costs of using nuclear weapons too great in relation to military effectiveness to make their use warranted? Can these political costs be reduced, or are they offset by the political costs of failing to make a stand?

These questions are answered in sharply different ways by the advocates of the two contrasting views of deterrence. As a result, each would establish the provocation threshold at grossly different points. The broad-deterrent view sets the provocation threshold at a low level, while reserving flexibility for the type and targeting of a nuclear response. A wide range of contingencies can thus be deterred by nuclear means. The narrow-deterrent view sets the threshold at a high point, thereby implying that a wide range of contingencies, varying with respect to geography, level of violence, duration and the Asian countries that may be involved, will remain irrelevant to the use of nuclear weapons and therefore undeterred.

Without attempting to be unrealistically precise about this fundamental question of provocation threshold, it is worth considering how it may be affected by the Chinese acquisition of nuclear capability. It is also pertinent to examine some of the contingencies in Asia that, wherever the threshold lies, will probably be below it. At a later stage in the chapter, a comment will be made about the intriguing, if perhaps academic, question of whether this threshold is higher in Asia or in Europe.

THE EFFECT OF A CHINESE CAPABILITY

On the matter of a Chinese nuclear capability, it is obvious that the question of provocation threshold is sensitive to the type of capability under consideration. For the next ten years a Chinese nuclear arsenal is likely to be quite limited in numbers of weapons, in delivery characteristics, and in its protection against pre-emptive attack—as limited, perhaps, as the planned French capability of about 150 weapons, each of about twenty kilotons, delivered by manned aircraft. Another estimate places the Chinese capability somewhat higher, to include a small number of medium-range missiles by 1970.[2] Clearly, the impact of such a Chinese capability is an extremely complex question, depending on many factors, including Sino-Soviet relations, the conditions that prevail in the rest of the world in and outside Asia, the preferences and pressures of allies, and, to some extent (although perhaps to a more limited extent than is frequently believed), the occupant of the White House. But if, in order to focus on the effect of a Chinese capability, one makes the possibly heroic assumption that these other factors remain about at their recent level, what can be said about the ensuing change, if any, in the provocation threshold? There are three logically possible effects that a Chinese nuclear capability might have on the provocation threshold.

First, it can be argued that a limited Chinese capability would have the paradoxical effect of *lowering* the threshold of provocation at which use of nuclear weapons against China would be effective and credible. The reasons for the paradox are both political and military. Chinese acquisition of a limited capability may accelerate the erosion of whatever protection remains from the Soviet "umbrella," thereby reducing the risk of Soviet involvement, and weakening one major source of military and political cost from the use of nuclear weapons against China. Furthermore, Chinese acquisition may lessen the antagonism felt inside and outside Asia at the possibility of a second use of nuclear weapons against targets in Asia. No doubt, the extent of this reaction would depend on China's own doctrine, declaratory policy, and behavior. If these were truculent, the political costs associated with use or threatened use of nuclear weapons against a nuclear-armed China may recede markedly. If, in seeking to exercise political leverage, a truculent China were to threaten to use its limited supply of weapons against *population* targets in countries supporting the United States and its allies, a United States threat to use nuclear weapons in

[2] See, for example, Ralph L. Powell, "China's Bomb: Exploitation and Reactions," *Foreign Affairs*, July 1965, p. 625; and Morton H. Halperin, "Chinese Nuclear Strategy: The Early Post-Detonation Period," *Adelphi Papers*, 18 (Institute of Strategic Studies), May 1965, p. 3.

a controlled manner against Chinese *military* targets could become morally less repugnant and politically more acceptable. Finally, the military gains from a first use of nuclear weapons against China might rise, because of the incentive to pre-empt against a small and vulnerable force that might otherwise do significant damage to United States or allied forces and installations in the area.

On the other hand, the complex calculation that might lead to the threshold-lowering effect may apply more to the world of academic strategy making than to crisis-conditioned decision making. Recognizing that decisions are made by particular actors in particular circumstances, the extra complexity and uncertainty that a Chinese nuclear capability would add to an already complex crisis might make an already perplexed and extended decision maker a little more cautious and reluctant than he would otherwise be. There might, of course, be the specific danger of a bomb detonated on a merchant ship in a United States harbor, or delivered by manned aircraft against a United States Pacific base, or launched by a Chinese submarine against a United States city or against an allied country; or of the healing of the Sino-Soviet rupture; or of the fearful clamor of exposed allies. But the greatest impact of a Chinese capability might simply be the added uncertainty that even a limited capability would create.

If one were to judge how decision makers *ought* to act, probably a stronger analytic case can be made for the threshold-*lowering* effect. But if one were to guess, instead, how decision makers are *likely* to act, the threshold-*raising* effect is perhaps more likely to ensue. Not that it would be great—there are obvious incentives for avoiding the use of nuclear weapons even in the absence of a Chinese capability— but if there is an effect at all, it will probably be one of accentuating the reluctance that would accompany any consideration of nuclear weapons use in Asia.

Finally, it can be argued that a Chinese capability would have a negligible effect on the provocation threshold. The case in support of this position can be readily inferred from the foregoing discussion. To the extent that decision makers seek to reduce their uncertainties, they may become more reluctant to employ nuclear weapons lest this expose them to a situation made more uncertain by Chinese possession of nuclear weapons. On the other hand, the possibly lowered political costs and increased military advantages of destroying a limited Chinese capability may create incentives to pre-empt. A balance between these forces may, plausibly, leave the provocation threshold unaffected.

THE DETERRED AND THE UNDETERRED

Consideration of specific contingencies leads to the conclusion that nuclear deterrence in Asia is by no means inapplicable or obsolete. It has its uses and functions as well as its limitations, and if we are sometimes keenly aware of its limitations in situations like those in Vietnam and Laos, we should nevertheless retain a lively sense of the relevance and utility which deterrence continues to have. If we fail to do so, we may become uncritically receptive to political solutions and arrangements that not only do not surmount the limitations of nuclear deterrence, but that compromise and vitiate its uses as well.

Three specific situations in which nuclear deterrence is powerfully operative are the cases of large-scale conventional (or nuclear) aggression against Korea, Taiwan, or Japan.[3] The two United States divisions in Korea—comparable in some respects to the United States force commitment in Western Europe—and the Seventh Fleet in the Straits of Formosa provide the trip-wire and the powder keg that make the possibility of a United States nuclear response an effective deterrent against such aggressions. In case this simple assertion be misunderstood, two clarifying points should be added. First, it is not being suggested that large-scale conventional aggression in either Korea or Taiwan would occur in the absence of nuclear deterrence. Surely, China has many other reasons for wanting to avoid or at least to postpone such confrontations. Not the least of these other reasons is that the conventional military forces in both areas are large and impressive; China's willingness and ability to mount the considerable effort and to incur the heavy costs of even a conventional response to

---

[3] Although most of the discussion of deterred conflicts is focused on conventional aggression, the credibility of United States deterrence applies *a fortiori* to the (unlikely) contingency of nuclear aggression by China against Korea, Taiwan, or Japan.

aggression must be limited. Nevertheless, by large-scale aggression against Korea or Taiwan, China would run the risk of United States nuclear strikes against military and high-value economic targets outside or inside China. This risk is sufficiently high to make these contingencies unlikely.

Second, the argument does not imply that Korean ground forces, and Chinese Nationalist ground and air forces in Taiwan, are unnecessary or of little value in view of the United States commitment and the residual danger of a first use of nuclear weapons. In both Korea and Taiwan, the existence of substantial conventional military capabilities retains considerable value. One reason is that such forces keep the conventional option open; under some circumstances, use of this option may be valuable. In addition, these forces also provide an asset that may be of use in deterring or meeting various conventional and "unconventional" contingencies *elsewhere* in Asia. Admittedly, we have not yet been too successful, or perhaps not sufficiently imaginative, in finding ways to make these assets usable elsewhere, a point to which we will return later.

Although the situation is different in Japan, the United States-Japanese treaty of 1960 and the presence in Japan of United States air forces certify a commitment that makes nuclear deterrence against any major attack on the Japanese islands (by either the Chinese or the Soviets) effective. Again, we do not suggest that a major attack would be likely to occur in the absence of the United States commitment. In fact, it is neither militarily nor politically plausible under present circumstances, quite apart from the United States guarantee. The point is simply that there remains a residual nuclear threat, and that it is a sufficiently powerful one to provide an effective deterrent in the foreseeable future, barring drastic changes within or outside Japan.

While there are thus a number of cases in which nuclear deterrence works, and is likely to continue to work, effectively, it is equally clear —and in the nature of the case, inevitable—that the situations that preoccupy us are the ones in which deterrence does not work and may not be relied upon to do so in the future. Laos and Vietnam are the two most critical examples; Indonesia's *"konfrontasi"* with Malaysia was a third. Still other examples of the ineffectuality, if not irrelevance, of nuclear deterrence arise in the Indian subcontinent in relation to recent and potential conflicts between India and Pakistan, and to the 1962 aggression by China against India. In possible future conflicts between India and China, however, the role of deterrence could become more prominent, especially since India has begun to alter its previous opposition to having such protection invoked in its behalf.

One of the principal reasons that there has been a growth in the likelihood and intensity of insurgency conflicts in Asia is the effectiveness of a possible nuclear response in deterring higher-scale provocations. Another explanation, of course, is that insurgency conflicts may simply be a more efficient technique for achieving communist objectives in the vulnerable, loosely integrated societies of most of the third world. In these conflicts, nuclear deterrence loses its credibility and relevance for many reasons, including the smallness of the provocation and the ambiguity of the aggressive act, springing from a tangle of internal as well as external motivations and support. It is true that the more we learn about these conflicts, the more important the external command-and-control function appears to be (*e.g.*, the control and support by the Lao Dong party in North Vietnam of the Viet Cong and the Pathet Lao). Nevertheless, there unquestionably remains an important element of *internal* volition, motivation, and organization, in both South Vietnam and Laos, which nurtures ambiguity and blurs the clear and present nature of the threat on which an effective and justifiable use of nuclear weapons depends.

From a military point of view, the result of insurgency conflicts is that there is not a well-defined battle line for locating appropriate tactical targets in the area of immediate operations. But the decisive limitation on nuclear deterrence in these situations is not military but political. In general, the political constraints are associated with a sharp disproportionality between the magnitude of a nuclear response and the level of violence in insurgent conflicts, as well as with the deep Asian animosity against another use of nuclear weapons on Asian targets. Moreover, a substantial component of the political costs of these insurgency conflicts might arise from an undesirable impact on Sino-Soviet relations: blurred Soviet commitments to respond in kind to pressure on China might thus be reactivated, and the deep split within the communist camp might be mended in the face of a common threat. Finally, the political costs that would accrue from the reactions of our allies outside Asia, as well as from reactions within the United States, combine to diminish the utility of nuclear weapons in these circumstances. As a consequence, the military benefits from using nuclear weapons are likely to be minimized, and the political costs maximized, in insurgency situations such as Vietnam and Laos.

In the other situations in which nuclear deterrence is largely inoperative (*e.g.*, the Indonesian confrontation with Malaysia, and the Indian-Pakistani frictions in Kashmir and the Rann of Kutch), most of the same constraints apply. In these cases, too, expected political costs from using nuclear weapons outweigh whatever limited military gains might be achieved. The reasons do not lie in the ambiguous source of the threat, as in Vietnam and Laos, but in the manifest disproportionality, the particular Asian sensitivity in this matter, and the possibly large and negative side effects in the rest of the world, in particular in connection with relations between the Soviet Union and China. Moreover, in most of these situations the ostensible military objectives of using nuclear weapons are probably achievable by conventional means, and at lower political costs.

The foregoing illustrations are useful in clarifying both the uses and the limitations of nuclear deterrence. However, we should avoid accepting a stable division between what is below and what is above the provocation threshold. For example, it is not too difficult to imagine circumstances—although they seem unlikely at the present time—in which the credibility of nuclear deterrence in Korea or Taiwan could be severely degraded. Internal disruption and disorder could lead to opportunities for external communist fomenting of insurgency, and the accompanying ambiguity of the threat, and its progress through gradually rising levels of violence, could blur the emergence of clear decision points, thereby rendering a nuclear threat disproportionate and irrelevant.

On the other hand, the Tonkin Gulf episode in August 1964 and the bombings of North Vietnam since February 1965 have suggested that an insurgency situation may escalate toward a conflict in which nuclear deterrence of further escalation could be credibly invoked—credibly enough to force not only an avoidance of further escalation, but perhaps some diminution of the original conflict as well. Situations on one side or the other of the provocation threshold can, by accident or intention, shift.

SOME PARALLELS TO
THE EUROPEAN SITUATION

Many of the situations we have been considering have counterparts in the European context. For example, in a rough and limited sense, Korea can be considered the West Germany of Asia. The substantial United States commitment of forces and weapons performs a roughly similar symbolic and trip-wire role in both countries. The substantial Korean forces also give considerable latitude for use of the conventional option. (In principle, the conventional forces of NATO provide a similar option in Germany.) Also, in a rough sense, Taiwan is the Berlin of Asia—or perhaps the analogy would be somewhat better between the offshore islands and Berlin. In both cases, it is the United States political commitment, rather than the presence of United States forces, that sustains the deterrent role.

In the European context, contingencies that are below the provocation threshold are perhaps more likely to arise in the southern flank than in the central front. (If in the central front, they are more likely to arise on the Soviet side than on the Western side.) It is no doubt true that the number and likelihood of military contingencies that are below the provocation threshold are much greater in Asia than in Europe. The reasons for this difference have already been discussed: the greater probability in the Asian context of insurgent situations, because of the unstable political, economic, and social environment; and the perhaps more sharply negative political effects from invoking nuclear weapons, because of the effect on Sino-Soviet relations and on Asian political orientations.

But is the provocation threshold lower in Asia than in Europe? One impressive factor tends to lower the threshold in the Asian context, and this is the markedly inferior and vulnerable Chinese military posture compared with that of the Soviet Union in Europe. (Nor is this likely to be seriously altered by Chinese acquisition of a nuclear capability of the dimensions previously discussed.) Failure to recognize this important difference between the Asian and European situations is one of the major weaknesses in the view, which is sometimes expressed in Europe and in Asia, that deterrence does not apply to Asia. With regard to Europe, this same view asserts that the United States deterrent is inoperative because (in the words of De Gaulle) the balance of deterrence between the Soviet Union and the United States "covers them directly but does not cover the other countries of the world." The proposed remedy for Western Europe is national nuclear forces. In Asia, essentially the same argument is made about the ineffectuality of both nuclear deterrence and other forms of United States military power, because of "the enormous risk of a general war" that the use of such power (*e.g.*, conventional military measures against North Vietnam) allegedly would entail. However, in the Asian context, political "neutralization" is advanced as the best prescription, given the failure of United States deterrent power, just as national nuclear forces are sometimes advanced as the best prescription, given the same alleged failure, in Western Europe. An exception to the Asian formula is occasionally made in behalf of Japan and India, for which, on technological and economic as well as military grounds, the European prescription—national nuclear forces—is advocated.[4]

While this argument has flaws in its European version, what is perhaps most curious is the stress that it places on the "enormous risk of a general war" as a barrier to applying military power effectively in Asia. Actually, the likelihood of general war arising from escalation of Asian conflicts is very much less, and the situation very much more stable in this respect, than the argument implies. Indeed, one might argue that this risk is so much less in Asia that the provocation threshold at which nuclear response is credible would be considerably lower in Asia than in Europe. (This is, of course, not an easy comparison to speculate about; one ought to take account, for example, of differences in the nature and depth of the United States commitment in NATO

---

[4] See, for example, General Gallois' interview with a Japanese correspondent in Paris, *Mainichi Shimbun*, January 20, 1964.

that might reverse this judgment. All things considered, however, one might conclude that the provocation threshold is likely to be lower in Asia than in Europe for the foreseeable future.)

CONCLUSION: PROBLEMS AND POLICIES IN SURMOUNTING THE LIMITATIONS OF DETERRENCE

In any event, the question of relative provocation thresholds is probably of secondary importance. In Asia we are left with a wide range of current and potential undeterred conflicts. Although nuclear deterrence is more effective than is often believed, its limitations are manifest not only in the Vietnamese and Laos cases, but in the unambiguous Indonesian confrontation with Malaysia from 1964 to 1966, and in the case of various forms of possible Chinese aggression against India or Burma. It is in this area of undeterred conflicts where our greatest need for improvements in programs and policies lies. The neutralization formula does not seem attractive because its laudable objectives (independence, security, nonintervention) lack the necessary means of assuring enforcement and maintaining stability. But the neutralization slogan at least underscores the necessity for finding measures and approaches that hold greater promise for arriving at acceptable and durable political-military solutions. In the rest of this chapter, our concern will be with some of the more promising lines of inquiry and innovation for developing better means to deal with undeterred conflicts in Asia.

One of the subjects on which it seems important to concentrate long-term attention is the matter of developing wider and more effective means of military, as well as economic and political, collaboration among the Asian countries themselves. The numerous political and ethnic obstacles to this objective are well known and serious, but the nature and importance of the problem warrant devoting more attention and imagination to it. We have usually thought that the large military forces built up in countries like Korea and Taiwan for historical reasons, and maintained for largely political reasons, have relevance only in World War II- or Korea-type conventional conflicts. In Asia, as we have seen, these are the types of conflicts which are very likely to be deterred. However, for *other* conflicts that may arise, the value and potential utility of these military assets have barely begun to be explored. The "more flags in Vietnam" policy, which has involved the use of appreciable Korean military units in South Vietnam, is a move in this direction.

To take one example from the preceding chapter, the many studies of counterinsurgency, unconventional warfare, and "modern warfare," based on British experience in Malaya, French experiences in Indochina and Algeria, and recent United States experience in Vietnam, emphasize the importance of a high ratio between counterinsurgent and insurgent forces. As noted earlier, numbers in this game are far from reliable; estimates of critical saturation ratios vary from 3 or 4 to 1 in the Philippines to over 20 to 1 in Malaya and Algeria. However, it seems evident that "clear and hold," "oil stain," or "strategic hamlet" operations in counterinsurgency campaigns are labor-intensive activities.

Part of the solution to meeting the threat of increasingly skillful insurgencies and other military threats in the Asian area may lie in measures to facilitate military collaboration within the region so that military forces can be built up rapidly when necessary without having to create and maintain large and expensive forces in all countries. Indeed, it might even be possible to accomplish this aim while bringing about some reductions in existing military forces. Actually, in the Asian arc from India to Korea and Japan, indigenous conventional military forces in the noncommunist countries considered together are only marginally inferior to the *total* conventional forces of China, North Vietnam, and North Korea. When United States forces in the Seventh Fleet and in the rest of the Pacific Command are added to the balance, the total conventional forces that are potentially available to the noncommunist countries probably *exceed* the aggregate strength of communist forces, excluding those of the Soviet Union, in the area. The problem is whether and how these *potential* forces might be made actually available for more flexible and effective use throughout the area.

Leaving political questions aside for the moment, this broad problem can be broken down into several sub-problems. Military forces in Asia differ widely in their relative cost and efficiency, probably by amounts as large as 3 or 4 to 1. Such differences suggest that substantial benefits, in terms of both lowered costs and increased capabilities, might be realized by some collaboration among countries and military forces in the area. Moreover, regional logistic arrangements for such services as aircraft and vehicle maintenance, and regional defense production in such fields as automotive and communications equipment, could result in economic benefits as well as in enhanced military effectiveness in the region as a whole.

In the short run, or even middle run, the development of a regional approach to security problems in Asia seems remote and unrealistic. There are tremendous obstacles: deep-seated cleavages, hostilities, divergent interests, and differences in world view among the noncommunist countries of the area. But the unexpected happens with surprising frequency in international affairs. The European Economic Community, for example, was an extremely remote possibility in 1946, and the Sino-Soviet rift surely seems much more understandable in 1966 than it would have in, say, 1950. In the case of Asian security problems, it is not inconceivable that ingenuity and effort, particularly if applied to some of the quasi-technical and politically less sensitive aspects of the problems, such as regional logistics and defense production, might gradually induce more significant and rapid progress toward regional collaboration in the years to come.

Of course, these comments should not be interpreted as advocating a purely military solution to insurgency and other security threats, which are admittedly basic political problems. The problem of regional security and regional military collaboration is only one aspect of the still broader problem of developing a regional political and economic, as well as military, counterweight to China. This prospect, too, is at best a long way in the future. But a network of nonmilitary regional institutions, with assistance from United States resources and with some improvement in military security in Southeast Asia, might begin to shape a new pattern in Asia. The possibilities are numerous, even though none alone is especially bright: a regional development bank for major capital projects in the area; a regional development authority in the Mekong valley; an Asian free trade area, and later perhaps a common market, with some special preferences and inducements granted by Japan to the less-developed member countries; an expansion of the ongoing and already effective multinational Asian Productivity Organization. In the economic as well as the military field, a gradual and narrow "project" approach that deliberately focuses on specific, technical collaborative ventures is more likely to bring results than is a broad "program" approach that seeks solutions in comprehensive treaties and alliances.

All these possibilities have been and are being studied, and all of them, as well as others, need further study as well as time to develop. None of them, nor all together, including regional military collaboration, would be a panacea in Asia any more than regional institutions have been a panacea in Europe. But the problems they are likely to leave—and to create—should be both more manageable and more congenial for the Asian countries and the United States than those which we currently face.

A final point is, in a sense, the European counterpart of the previous point about the desirability of expanding regional collaboration among the Asian countries. Present prospects do not appear bright for attempting to move in the direction of what has sometimes been referred to as a "common foreign policy" for NATO, especially with respect to conflict and coexistence in Asia. Nevertheless, there may be more opportunities than have been so far exploited for a closer relationship between the United States and its European allies on matters relating to Asia, and between the European NATO members and the Asian countries as well. Such opportunities extend beyond the "more flags in Vietnam" policy, to a closer consultative and collaborative effort in general on these matters. A sharing of views should be accompanied by some further sharing of the aid burden on the military aspects of the problem no less than on the economic development aspects. Britain, of course, is already deeply involved in these problems through a sharing of the burdens and responsibilities in Malaysia and in India, although the durability of these commitments is subject to question. President de Gaulle is right in saying that now that the European countries have "rebuilt their economy and are in the process of rebuilding their military strength," they should be capable of assuming responsibilities which they have not been able to assume in the past two decades. It should be both possible and desirable to explore ways in which various European countries might assume part of the burden in Asia, and in the process contribute to a better mutual understanding between the United States and its European allies and to closer collaboration in the conduct of their policies and programs.

Part
Two

EMPIRICAL ASPECTS OF POLITICAL, MILITARY, AND ECONOMIC RELATIONSHIPS

Part
Two

Introduction to Part Two

In the following chapters, we turn to examine a number of specific problems and hypotheses bearing on United States programs and policies. Part Two is more diversified and technical than the preceding chapters, and the methods used are, in contrast to Part One, frequently quantitative. The principal aim in Part Two is to test various hypotheses bearing on relationships between policies and programs, and between them and the objectives they seek to accomplish.

In exploring these relationships, frequent reference will be made to the general discussion of Part One. However, the primary aim is to formulate hypotheses that can be tested against available data. The availability of data frequently determines the particular region or country with which the discussion is concerned. Thus, Chapters Five and Six concentrate on Latin America for this reason, while Chapter Seven deals with Vietnam and Iran, and Chapter Eight uses data from a large number of less-developed countries spread throughout the third world.

A general comment about the altered focus of Part Two should be added. Most of the chapters in Part Two have resulted from studies that tried to deal quantitatively with several broad problems, policies, and programs. But these studies confronted a basic and familiar difficulty. While the problems are broad and complex, the data available for testing hypotheses are quite limited, both in scope and reliability. The result is that empirical work usually has to focus on a piece of a broad problem, rather than on the entire problem. This is not an argument against empiricism. It is simply a reminder that the added depth that empirical work can sometimes bring to understanding a problem usually has to be bought at a price of narrowing the problem.

CHAPTER
FIVE

Military Programs and Political Effects: Some Indications from Latin America

The political effects of military programs, like those of economic development programs, are hard to unravel for reasons that are powerful and familiar.[1] In the first place, political effects are themselves difficult to identify, let alone to measure. The kinds of political changes that we can observe directly are usually the sharp, discontinuous changes: a coup or a revolution, an outbreak of guerrilla activity, a new constitution, the signing of a treaty or alliance agreement. Even in such cases, the apparent meaning of a change may be deceptive, or the change itself short-lived. Gradual changes in the extent of public participation in politics, in the degree of competitiveness in the political arena, in attitudes and preferences on foreign policy and defense issues, are usually still more ambiguous and more difficult to observe accurately.

Furthermore, political effects may be plausibly attributable to many causes—to so many, in fact, that the role of any single cause becomes highly conjectural. If a military coup occurs, for example, is it to be

---

[1] As used here, "military programs" refers both to military aid programs (MAP) from the United States and to domestic defense programs.

explained by the increased strength or size of the defense establishment, or by its impoverishment; by the resistance of a conservative elite to the process or threat of change, or by the impatience of a modernizing elite at the rigidity, venality, or ineffectuality of the civilian government; by personal animosities between military and civilian leaders, or by conflicts within the military itself; by too rapid a rate of economic and social change, or by not enough change? Not only may there be many possible explanations, but we are frequently confronted by the plausibility of opposites.

A further difficulty arises from the fact that the connection between a possible cause, on the one hand, and the military program, on the other, is often hard to establish. Even if we think we know which cause applies in a certain case, it is by no means evident how much of a role has been played by a particular military aid program or domestic defense program.

Because of the difficulties of accurate observation and the multiplicity of plausible causes, it is easier to formulate broad and simple assertions about causal relationships than it is to dispel them. This chapter will examine one set of such assertions about the political effects of military programs in less-developed countries. Data on Latin America will be used to test some of the hypotheses that seem to be implicit in these assertions.

Thus, we shall rediscover the truism that it is unwise and unwarranted to offer simple explanations for complicated phenomena. If this conclusion seems bland, it should be remembered that eliminating easy misunderstanding is often a prerequisite to arriving at better understanding.

SOME VIEWS OF POLITICAL-MILITARY INTERACTIONS

Public discussion of political effects of military programs in the third world has concentrated on the effects of United States military aid programs in particular, rather than of the countries' over-all defense programs, largely because such discussion has usually been connected with congressional consideration of military aid programs. One of the central themes in this discussion has been that such programs tend to be associated with repressive, authoritarian, and dictatorial governments that are under military control or have distinctly military overtones.

THE EROSION-OF-DEMOCRACY VIEW

There are several variations of this central theme. One view holds that military aid will increase the threat of overt military takeover or of covert military control of the political process. Military influence or intervention in the politics of developing countries is presumed to be repressive, and is also presumed to increase as a result of military assistance provided by the United States, often leading ultimately to direct military takeover. This view was stated by Senator Fulbright in the Senate Hearings on the Foreign Assistance Act of 1961 as follows:

> It is true, is it not, that three of the countries which have received the largest amount of our military aid—outside of the Western European countries—Turkey, Pakistan and Korea, have all had military coups supplanting a civilian government, and now are under what could be called a military dictatorship. . . .
> I was wondering whether there is any relationship here between these events and the extent of our military aid. This is in contrast to one other country that has been a heavy recipient of non-military aid. I speak of India . . . in which there has been a relatively stable, civilian administration throughout this period, and the reports are that it is making considerable progress.[2]

And again:

> How do you explain this unusual coincidence that countries where you put the most military aid—the underdeveloped countries, not Germany, France, or developed countries—are the very ones who have lost their civilian governments . . . ?[3]

The point was echoed by Senator Aiken:

[2] United States Senate, *International Development and Security*, Hearings, Committee on Foreign Relations, 87th Congress, First Session, Part II, May 1961, pp. 610–612.
[3] *Ibid.*, p. 681.

The experience of some of these countries has been that when they get a strong military force, the military just takes over.[4]

Essentially the same point, though this time relating to defense expenditures generally rather than to United States military aid in particular, was also made by Senator Fulbright in the Senate Hearings:

The only point is that these big military expenditures do not contribute to political stability or economic growth. On the contrary, they contribute to the creation of a military dictatorship. . . . The countries where there have been the biggest military programs all seem to turn up with a military dictatorship.[5]

An editorial in *The New York Times* endorsed this view with particular reference to Latin America:

The countries in Latin America which are most stable and most democratic, such as Uruguay, Costa Rica and Mexico, spend little or almost nothing on military defense. Arms only encourage right-wing military dictatorships.[6]

Various explanations are offered of the process that leads to the erosion of civilian control and its replacement by repressive military authority. One theory is that military programs simply contribute to increasing the absolute and relative powers of the military elite, thereby changing the internal pattern of political checks and balances, and replacing it with a new relationship in which the military has predominance. As Frank Tannenbaum formulates it:

The arming of the central government's forces upset the traditional bridling of tyranny at the center and made it impossible for anyone to overthrow the government except the army, which means that no one can be elected or keep office unless he is acceptable to the army. All of civilian government (or nearly all) is at the mercy of the army.[7]

[4] *Ibid.*, p. 669.
[5] *Ibid.*, p. 732. Similar views have also been expressed by H. L. Matthews; for example, in "When Generals Take Over in Latin America," *The New York Times Magazine*, September 9, 1962, p. 144.
[6] *The New York Times*, June 13, 1961. Quoted in Seymour Melman, *The Peace Race*, New York, George Braziller, 1961, pp. 58–59.
[7] Frank Tannenbaum, "Considerations for the Latin American Policy," in James Roosevelt (ed.), *The Liberal Papers*, New York, Doubleday and Co., Inc., 1962, p. 281.

Another theory of the erosion-of-democracy process holds that the effect of large military programs is less direct. Large programs will lead to still larger programs; and the result is to "overburden a country with expenditures it cannot support," leading to inflation, political instability, and the erosion of civilian government largely as a result of financial and other internal difficulties.[8]

Whichever theory of the process is adopted, the result is essentially similar. The implication is that the greater the quantity of military aid, the greater the erosion of civilian and competitive political institutions, and their replacement by military and authoritarian controls. If we assume that the relationship is continuous rather than discrete,[9] it follows that political institutions would become more tightly controlled and authoritarian as military aid grows—or more generally, as the size of the military establishment and its claim on resources increase. This view suggests that relatively large military programs will be associated with relatively large political shifts toward authoritarianism and away from democracy.

THE SUPPORT-FOR-AUTHORITARIANISM VIEW

Another version of the connection between military programs and political consequences focuses on the *types* of regimes that desire and require military programs. This view suggests not that military aid and other military programs *lead* toward authoritarian regimes (the erosion-of-democracy view), but that authoritarian regimes—however they come into being—generate relatively large demands for military assistance and defense budgets. In this view, the connection between military and political factors takes a different form. Military programs do not necessarily create authoritarian regimes, or increase the probability of their occurrence. Instead, such regimes generate a relatively large demand for military programs. Again, assuming that the relationship is continuous rather than discrete, this support-for-authori-

---

[8] United States Senate, *International Development and Security*, Hearings, *op. cit.*, p. 681. The quotation is from Senator Fulbright's interrogation of Secretary McNamara, and referred specifically to Turkey. A similar view, relating to South and Southeast Asia, is expressed by Vera Micheles Dean, "Southeast Asia and Japan," in *The Liberal Papers, op. cit.*, pp. 267–268.

[9] That is, if we assume that political effects grow with the size of the program.

tarianism view suggests that large military programs will be associated with less democratic and more authoritarian regimes.

Reasoning along this line led to the restriction contained in the foreign aid legislation against providing military aid in Latin America for 'internal security purposes" except in case of a special presidential determination to the contrary.[10] Underlying this view has been a feeling that internal security requirements, particularly in Latin America, are generally of moderate size and easily within each country's financial capabilities. Where such requirements become sufficiently large to generate a need for United States military aid, the presumption is that the regime requiring the aid is probably repressive, dictatorial, and reactionary. The view was expressed, for example, by Senator Carlson in the Senate Hearings on foreign aid in 1962:

> Is it not true that in many of the Latin American countries they are either military dictatorships or other dictatorships, and with our military assistance programs, and probably other programs, we maintain the governments in power?
> . . . I am concerned about our Nation, through military assistance and Federal funds maintaining governments that I do not believe would be classed as democratic or representative of the people.[11]

A similar belief was advanced by David Scull, a member of the policy committee of the Society of Friends:

> I would like to record our conviction that military assistance . . . determined primarily by military considerations, often bolstered totalitarian dictatorships which may have as many unpleasant characteristics as any Communist regime. . . . I know that members of this Committee have expressed concern over the possible misuse of military aid to Latin America. We Friends would be pleased indeed if such aid were ended. . . .[12]

[10] See, for example, the comments by Senator Morse in United States Senate, *International Development and Security*, Hearings, *op. cit.*, pp. 618–620; and along similar lines in United States Senate, *Foreign Assistance Act of 1962*, Hearings, Committee on Foreign Relations, 87th Congress, 2nd Session, April 1962, pp. 420–421.

[11] United States Senate, *Foreign Assistance Act of 1962*, Hearings, *op. cit.*, pp. 76–77.

[12] *Ibid.*, p. 490.

The New York Times advanced the same view in the 1961 editorial previously referred to:

> Representative O'Hara . . . put his finger on the main objection to the proposed policy [of enlarged military aid to Latin America] when he said that the Pentagon is asking for "a blank check from Congress to maintain governments in power"; they can be strong only if cherished in the minds and hearts of the people.[13]

Similar hypotheses about military aid were expressed earlier in *The Nation* by Stanley Meisler:

> In most cases, military aid . . . has tended (1) to force weak nations into devoting huge percentages of their vital capital to armaments; (2) to *entrench undemocratic, military governments*; and (3) to promote arms races between the governments.[14]

The reasoning behind the support-for-authoritarianism view can be summarized as follows: (a) military aid helps to keep recipient governments in power; (b) dictatorships, oligarchies, or otherwise unrepresentative and anti-reformist governments are more difficult to keep in power than are democratic and representative governments; (c) therefore, reactionary governments desire and require relatively larger military expenditures and military aid; (d) hence, the size of military aid and other military programs in such countries will tend to be relatively large. In expressions of the support-for-authoritarianism hypothesis, the operative words are "maintain," "support," "bolster." By contrast, the operative words in the erosion-of-democracy hypothesis are "takeover," "military coup," "creation of dictatorship."

TESTING THE HYPOTHESES
WITH LATIN AMERICAN DATA

In this section our aim is to test in a rough way the erosion-of-democracy and the support-for-authoritarianism views of the connections between military programs and political effects. The tests are admit-

[13] *The New York Times*, June 13, 1961, quoted in Seymour Melman, *op. cit.*, p. 58.
[14] *The Nation*, Vol. 190, No. 16, April 16, 1960, p. 334. Italics added.

tedly crude, both because of the difficulty of the problem itself and because of the limitations of the available data. The tests are confined to Latin America because a unique set of data on political development over the last decade is available for that region. From these data it is possible to rank the Latin American countries according to (1) the *level* of political democracy, and (2) the *change* in this level relative to the other Latin American countries over the period 1950 to 1960. The tests will consist of comparing these political indicators with two additional sets of data—figures on total and per capita United States military aid programs, and on the domestic military budgets in these countries—to see whether the asserted relationships actually appear.

THE DATA

The political data that we will use are based upon work done over the past fifteen years by Russell H. Fitzgibbon, professor of political science and formerly director of the Center for Latin American Studies at the University of California at Los Angeles.[15] On four occasions, in 1945, 1950, 1955, and 1960, Fitzgibbon conducted a survey among specialists on Latin America to elicit from them an evaluation of the political climate in the individual Latin American countries. Each of the respondents was asked to rate twenty Latin American countries according to fifteen political, social, and economic criteria, using a five-point rating scale for each criterion. The criteria included freedom of elections, of the press, of party organization, and independence of judicial processes. Also included were several criteria that are possibly less directly relevant for measuring political democracy, relating to educational level, standard of living, and "a sense of internal unity and national cohesion." Although one criterion dealt explicitly with

[15] See Russell H. Fitzgibbon and Kenneth F. Johnson, "Measurement of Latin American Political Change," *American Political Science Review*, Vol. 55, No. 3, September 1961, pp. 515–526; Russell H. Fitzgibbon, "How Democratic is Latin America?" *Inter-American Economic Affairs*, Vol. 9, No. 4, Spring 1956, pp. 65–77; "A Statistical Evaluation of Latin American Democracy," *Western Political Quarterly*, Vol. 9, No. 3, September 1956, pp. 607–619; and "Measurement of Latin American Political Phenomena: A Statistical Experiment," *American Political Science Review*, Vol. 45, No. 2, June 1951, pp. 517–523.

civilian supremacy over the military, this was not the main focus of the survey. Instead, its main concern was to evaluate the institutions and practices in each country "according to a scale of political change relevant to democracy."[16]

The responses of each subject were adjusted by a proportional method (so that each respondent's total scores for all countries would amount to 1,000 points, compared with a theoretical maximum of 1,700), in order to offset subjective differences between optimists and pessimists. In the tests discussed here, the adjusted scores are the basis for a ranking of countries according to their "level" of political development at a given point in time. Changes in the ranking of individual countries are used as a basis for judging the direction of political change over time.

There are many shortcomings in the Fitzgibbon method and data, including the ambiguity and heterogeneity of the criteria, the weights applied to them (the criterion relating to free elections was given twice the weight of most of the others; freedom of the press, a weight half again as large), and the qualifications and prejudices of the respondents (nearly all were from the United States). Some of these difficulties could be overcome by independent work with the original raw data.[17] In this chapter, however, we confine the analysis to Fitzgibbon's own results as they stand, without modifications. In spite of their limitations, the Fitzgibbon data represent a pioneering and useful effort in a field whose complexity is equaled by its importance. Moreover, the variance tests performed on the Fitzgibbon data strongly suggest that they are statistically meaningful. (These tests are described in Appendix A.)

Table 5-1 summarizes the Fitzgibbon data that we have used. Column 7 shows the sum of the scores given to each country by all respondents during three survey periods: 1950, 1955, and 1960.

---

[16] Fitzgibbon and Johnson, op. cit., p. 516.

[17] For example, it would be possible to separate out responses to the more distinctly relevant and unambiguous criteria, and those of the more qualified respondents, and to change the weights. It should also be possible to compare the subjective estimates of the respondents with objective data relating to the courts, educational practices and school attendance, press circulation, the frequency and character of elections, and so on.

In the statistical tests described below, column 8 from Table 5-1 (the ranking of countries according to their total scores on the three surveys) is used as a crude measure of each country's relative level of political democracy over the 1950–1960 period. To obtain a rough measure of the change in political level relative to other countries, column 9, is used, showing the difference in each country's rank between the 1950 and 1960 surveys. As column 9 indicates, five countries showed no change, while seven countries moved up or down by just one rank. We therefore use change in rank only to establish a dichotomous grouping of countries in terms of whether their rank did or did not rise. A rise in rank between 1950 and 1960 indicates that the country became more democratic, as measured by the Fitzgibbon rankings, relative to the other Latin American countries.[18] The "rise-no rise" grouping is then compared with a dichotomous grouping of the military aid data, classified in terms of whether the size of military programs did or did not exceed the median.

The data on total and per capita military aid programs in Latin America for the 1950–1960 period are summarized in Table 5-2.

MILITARY AID AND LEVEL OF DEMOCRACY

The first hypothesis to be tested—a variant of the support-for-authoritarianism view—concerns the association between the total amount of aid under the Military Assistance Program (MAP) and level of political development as indicated by the total Fitzgibbon scores. Spearman's rank correlation coefficient, r_s, was computed from the MAP ranking shown in column 2 of Table 5-2 and the political-level ranking shown in column 8 of Table 5-1. The coefficient is .2654, which is not significantly different from zero at a 25 per cent level of

18 The method used thus focuses on political change in relation to the other countries, rather than on the absolute change in the Fitzgibbon score, which would be indicated by comparing column 1 and column 5. This method seems preferable because the technique used by Fitzgibbon in normalizing the point scores of respondents had the effect of making the "value" of a point in 1950 slightly different from that in 1960. Hence, changes in absolute scores between the two surveys might be misleading. However, as a check on the results obtained from our dichotomous-grouping method, we also examined changes in absolute scores. The check confirmed the results that were obtained with the dichotomous groupings.

TABLE 5-1 *Fitzgibbon Indexes of Political Development for Latin America, 1950, 1955, 1960*
(adjusted scores from specialists' responses to questionnaires[a])

COUNTRY	1950		1955		1960		INDEX OF POLITICAL DEVELOPMENT (SUM OF ADJUSTED SCORES COLUMNS 1+3+5)	CHANGE IN RANK ORDER 1950–1960	
	RATING POINTS (1)	RANK (2)	RATING POINTS (3)	RANK (4)	RATING POINTS (5)	RANK (6)	(7)	RANK (8)	(COLUMN 2 – COLUMN 6)[c] (9)
Argentina	542	8	513	7	652	4	1707	7	4
Bolivia	335	17	384	15	406	16	1125	15	1
Brazil	612	5	651	5	600	7	1863	4	–2
Chile	740	2	735	3	688	3	2163	3	–1
Colombia	602	6	524	6	602	6	1728	6	0
Costa Rica	713	3	773	2	713	2	2199	2	1
Cuba[b]	[667]	[4]	[513]	[7]	[422]	[14]	[1602]	—	[–10][d]
Dominican Republic	318	19	312	19	290	18	920	18	1
Ecuador	479	9	498	10	514	10	1491	8	–1
El Salvador	422	14	469	11	468	12	1359	11	2
Guatemala	478	10	398	14	445	13	1321	12.5	–3
Haiti	331	18	375	17	283	19	989	17	–1
Honduras	378	15	426	12	414	15	1218	14	0
Mexico	570	7	657	4	613	5	1840	5	2
Nicaragua	351	16	336	18	341	17	1028	16	–1
Panama	468	11	505	9	478	11	1451	9	0
Paraguay	293	20	297	20	261	20	851	19	0
Peru	425	13	378	16	518	9	1321	12.5	4
Uruguay	804	1	850	1	767	1	2421	1	0
Venezuela	448	12	404	13	564	8	1416	10	4

Source: Russell H. Fitzgibbon and Kenneth F. Johnson, "Measurement of Latin American Political Change," American Political Science Review, Vol. 55, No. 3, September 1961, p. 518.

Notes

[a] Fitzgibbon describes the scores as comprising "a scale of political change relevant to democracy." The scores are based on the weighted ratings given to 15 criteria of political development by 10, 20, and 40 respondents in 1950, 1955, and 1960, respectively. Fitzgibbon adjusted the raw scores to allow for differences in optimism or pessimism of the respondents, and for changes in the number of respondents in each poll. See text discussion, pp. 97–99.

[b] The point scores for Cuba are included for comparability, but excluded from the rankings because the available data on U.S. military aid and Cuban defense expenditures with which the political scores are to be compared cover the period from 1950 through the middle of 1958 only, and hence are not comparable to the corresponding military data for the other Latin American countries, which extend through 1960.

[c] A positive figure indicates that the country's rank among the Latin American countries, in terms of its adjusted political development score, rose by the number of places shown between 1950 and 1960. A movement from tenth place in 1950 to sixth place in 1960 would be shown as 4. If columns 2 and 6 are renumbered to exclude Cuba, a few changes occur in column 9. For example, Brazil changes from −2 to −3, and Colombia from 0 to −1. However, none of the resulting changes affects the "rise-no rise" grouping of the column 9 entries.

[d] The decline in Cuba's rank by 10 is based on a 20-country ranking for 1950 and 1960.

TABLE 5-2   *Military Assistance in Latin America, 1950–1960*

COUNTRY	TOTAL MAP (1950–1960 IN MILLIONS OF DOLLARS)[a] (1)	RANK (2)	MAP PER CAPITA (1950–1960, DOLLARS)[b] (3)	RANK (4)
Argentina	0.07	16	0.003	18
Bolivia	0.44	14	0.14	14
Brazil	164.8	1	2.82	7
Chile	48.1	3	7.11	2
Colombia	30.6	4	2.37	8
Costa Rica	0.005	18	0.005	17
Cuba[c]	[16.0]	—	[2.61]	—
Dominican Republic	8.0	8	3.17	6
Ecuador	18.7	7	5.07	4
El Salvador	0.02	17	0.009	16
Guatemala	1.1	12	0.34	11
Haiti	2.0	10	0.17	13
Honduras	0.82	13	0.49	10
Mexico	3.2	9	0.11	15
Nicaragua	1.4	11	1.12	9
Panama	0	19	0	19
Paraguay	0.36	15	0.23	12
Peru	50.9	2	5.42	3
Uruguay	24.0	5	9.18	1
Venezuela	21.6	6	3.74	5

Source: Department of Defense, Director of Military Assistance, *Military Assistance Programs—Programs and Deliveries, Fiscal Years 1950–1961*, Washington, D. C., May 1961.

Notes

[a] Total military aid program (MAP) includes grant aid, credit assistance, and deliveries from excess stocks.

[b] Population figures used in per capita calculations are estimates for 1955 from United Nations, *Demographic Yearbook 1959*, New York, 1960.

[c] Equipment deliveries to Cuba were ended in March 1958. The Cuba figures are included for general interest, but excluded from the rank-order comparisons because the MAP deliveries are for a shorter period than in the other countries.

significance.[19] The assertion that the total amount of military aid is unrelated to authoritarianism cannot be rejected. In fact, the positive

[19] The significance of r_s was tested by the value of t, where:

$$t = r_s \sqrt{[N - 2]/[1 - r_s^2]}$$

with N−2 degrees of freedom, and N=19. A two-tailed test was used on the sign of the rank correlation coefficient provides some support (although it is weak) for a conjecture that the amount of military aid is positively associated with level of political *democratization.*[20]

The second hypothesis in the support-for-authoritarianism view concerns the association between military aid *per capita* and level of political democracy. Spearman's coefficient (computed from the per capita MAP ranks shown in Table 5-2, column 4, and the political-level ranks shown in Table 5-1, column 8) is .1285, which is not significantly different from zero at a 50 per cent level.[21] The assertion that the amount of military aid per capita is unrelated to the level of political development in Latin America cannot be rejected.

MILITARY AID AND CHANGE IN POLITICAL LEVEL

The next hypotheses are related to the erosion-of-democracy theme, and are concerned with the association between *change* in relative political ranking and, successively, (a) total MAP, and (b) MAP per capita. To test the degree of association, we use the Fisher exact-probability test. The test determines whether the two groups from one sample differ in the proportion with which they fall into the two classes of the other.[22]

To measure change in political position, the Latin American countries are divided into two groups: those whose level of political development rose relative to the other countries (Group A), and those

---

assumption of a null hypothesis that r_s is not different from zero. (See Sidney Siegel, *Non-Parametric Statistics for the Behavioral Sciences*, New York, McGraw-Hill, 1956, pp. 210–212.)

[20] If some of the previously cited conjectures were accepted (see above, pp. 92–96), we should expect that a higher rank in the amount of military aid would be associated with a lower rank in the scale of political development. In this case, the null hypothesis would be that r_s is not different from zero, and the alternative hypothesis that r_s is *less* than zero. Here a one-tailed test would be appropriate. To reject the null hypothesis (in favor of the alternative hypothesis) at a significance level of 10 per cent, r_s would have to be < -1.333. Actually, with the present data, $r_s = +.2654$ and $t = +1.1331$, which provides more support for an alternative hypothesis to the effect that higher MAP rank is associated with a higher level of political development.

[21] Again, a two-tailed t-test was used.

[22] The Fisher test is a useful nonparametric test for the degree of association between two independent samples where the sample size is small (less than 20), and where the observations from each sample fall into one of two mutually exclusive classes. See Siegel, *op. cit.*, pp. 96–104.

whose relative political level did not rise (Group B). According to the changes in ranking shown in Table 5-1, column 9, eight countries are in Group A and eleven in Group B.[23]

For comparative purposes, the Latin American countries are also divided into two groups according to their total MAP: those for which military aid from 1950 to 1960 exceeded the median (Group I), and those for which military aid did not exceed the median (Group II). Similarly, the figures on per capita military aid are the basis for a distinction between those countries above the median (Group III), and those not above the median (Group IV). Given a unique median, there are obviously nine countries in Group I (and Group III), and ten countries in Group II (and Group IV).

First, consider the comparison between countries grouped according to change in political ranking, and countries grouped according to military aid.[24] If there were a close connection between change in political rank and military aid, we would expect that the countries receiving relatively more military aid (Group I) would also be those whose political rank did not rise (Group B), and the countries receiving relatively less military aid (Group II) would also be those whose political rank rose (Group A). Instead, we find that countries with relatively high military aid included almost an equal number of those whose political rank rose (Peru, Venezuela, Dominican Republic, and Mexico) and of those whose political rank did not rise (Uru-

[23] Group A: Argentina, Bolivia, Costa Rica, Dominican Republic, El Salvador, Mexico, Peru, Venezuela.

Group B: Brazil, Chile, Colombia, Ecuador, Guatemala, Haiti, Honduras, Nicaragua, Panama, Paraguay, Uruguay. Group B includes both those countries whose rank fell, and those whose rank did not change.

As an alternative, the countries were grouped into those whose political rank fell relative to the other Latin American countries (Group B'), and those whose political rank did not fall (Group A'). In this dichotomy, countries whose rank did not change between 1950 and 1960 (Colombia, Honduras, Panama, Paraguay, and Uruguay, as shown in Table 5-1, column 9, were included in Group A', along with countries whose rank rose. Thus, the relationship between political change and military programs was tested with the "fall" versus "no fall," as well as the "rise" versus "no rise," dichotomy. Only the latter results are reported here because the unrelatedness between change in political level and size of military program persists in every case for both types of groupings.

[24] Appendix Table B-1 shows the distribution of countries according to the political change dichotomy compared with the military aid dichotomy.

guay, Brazil, Chile, Ecuador, and Colombia). Similarly, countries with relatively less military aid included nearly an equal number of those whose political rank rose (Bolivia, El Salvador, Costa Rica, and Argentina) and of those whose political rank did not rise (Nicaragua, Honduras, Guatemala, Paraguay, Haiti, and Panama). Actually, the distribution of countries is so evenly balanced that one cannot reject the assertion that there is *no* association between the two groupings.[25]

Next, consider the comparison between a grouping according to change in political rank, and a grouping according to military aid per capita.[26] Once again we find that countries with relatively high military aid per capita include countries whose relative political standing improved (Peru, Venezuela, and the Dominican Republic) as well as countries whose political standing did not improve (Uruguay, Chile, Ecuador, Brazil, Colombia, and Nicaragua). Similarly, countries with relatively low military aid per capita include countries whose political rank rose (Mexico, Bolivia, El Salvador, Costa Rica, and Argentina) as well as countries whose political rank did not rise (Honduras, Guatemala, Paraguay, Haiti, and Panama). Again the distribution of countries over the two dichotomies is sufficiently evenly balanced that it is not possible to reject the assertion that there is *no* association between the grouping according to per capita military aid and the grouping according to change in relative political standing.[27]

DEFENSE EXPENDITURES AND POLITICAL LEVEL

The hypotheses so far considered have been concerned with the relationship between military aid data and the Fitzgibbon political indexes. But military aid comprises only part of the resources devoted to military establishments in the Latin American countries, and generally a small part at that. In fact, for the fourteen Latin American

25 According to the Fisher test, the exact probability of occurrence of frequencies distributed as evenly as those in Appendix Table B-1, or more *unevenly*, is 60 per cent, *if there were no relationship between military aid grouping and political change grouping.*

26 The distribution of countries according to the two dichotomies is shown in Appendix Table B-2.

27 The probability of occurrence of a distribution as even as, or more uneven than, that in Appendix Table B-2 is 39.5 per cent, *if there were no relationship between the two groupings.*

countries for which unclassified data are available on domestic defense budgets during the 1950–1960 period, total defense expenditures annually averaged about twenty-five times more than the average annual amount of military aid. Table 5-3 shows average annual per capita defense expenditures for these countries, expressed in 1960 United States dollars.

The data in Table 5-3 are of interest apart from the specific purposes for which we have introduced them. For example, the per capita figures show that the highest annual per capita defense expenditures have been in Venezuela (since 1958 a relatively liberal, if troubled, country under the leadership of Betancourt and Leoni), whereas the second-from-lowest per capita defense outlays over the 1950–1960 period were in Duvalier's Haiti. Evidently, a strongly repressive regime can get along without much military equipment. Billy clubs can be used to support a repressive, dictatorial regime, while tanks and automatic weapons may be needed to protect a democratic regime from the use of organized terror and violence against it. It is also noteworthy that annual data for Venezuela indicate that total and per capita defense expenditures have been as high under Betancourt and Leoni as they were at the end of the repressive regime of Perez Jimenez in 1957–1958.

Relationships that do not seem to apply to military aid might nevertheless apply to domestic military programs. It is therefore worthwhile to investigate whether there appears to be an association between political development indicators and defense expenditures in Latin America, even though no such association appeared in the case of military aid and political development. Hence, we shall reconsider the support-for-authoritarianism and the erosion-of-democracy hypotheses, but with defense expenditure data substituted for those on military aid.

The data and rankings on defense expenditures in Table 5-3 are compared with the Fitzgibbon political development measures from Table 5-1 for the fourteen relevant countries.[28] Because of data limi-

[28] Country rankings, columns 8 and 9 in Table 5-1, were recalculated to exclude Uruguay, the Dominican Republic, Nicaragua, Paraguay, and Panama, for which data on defense outlays were not available. Subsequent computations are based on the fourteen remaining countries.

TABLE 5-3 *Average Annual Defense Expenditures for*
Latin American Countries, 1950–1960

(in 1960 U.S. dollars)[a]

COUNTRY	AVERAGE ANNUAL DEFENSE EXPENDITURES, 1950–1960 (IN MILLIONS)	RANK	AVERAGE ANNUAL PER CAPITA DEFENSE EXPENDITURES, 1950–1960 (DOLLARS PER CAPITA)	RANK
Argentina	234.82	2	13.43	3
Bolivia[b]	3.34	13	1.03	14
Brazil	265.46	1	4.50	5
Chile[c]	104.58	4	14.88	2
Colombia	60.55	6	3.88	6
Costa Rica	1.73	14	1.78	12
Ecuador	14.33	8	3.71	7
El Salvador	5.89	10	2.63	8
Guatemala	6.93	9	2.09	11
Haiti	5.26	11	1.57	13
Honduras	3.73	12	2.25	9
Mexico[d]	68.79	5	2.14	10
Peru	49.85	7	5.26	4
Venezuela	107.64	3	17.97	1

Sources: For defense expenditures in local currency at current prices: United Nations, *Statistical Yearbook* (volumes for 1954 through 1961). For price indexes and dollar exchange rates: the source quoted above plus International Monetary Fund, *International Financial Statistics* (monthly); and Agency for International Development, *Regional Data Book for Latin America,* Washington, D. C., Office of Statistics and Reports, 1962. For population data: United Nations, *Demographic Yearbook 1960,* New York, 1961.

Notes
[a] Defense expenditures in current prices were converted to 1960 U.S. dollars, using price indexes based on 1960 as the deflator, and 1960 official dollar exchange rates. No attempt is made to adjust for possible overvaluation of local currencies.
[b] Based on annual figures for 1953, 1955, 1956, and 1957 only.
[c] Based on annual figures for 1953–1960 only.
[d] Based on annual figures for 1955–1960 only.

tations, five countries had to be omitted, including three that had highly repressive and authoritarian regimes during the 1950–1960 period. Consequently, the results obtained from the fourteen-country tests should be treated with particular caution.

We will first test the association between average annual defense expenditures and level of political democratization, as indicated by the rank ordering according to the Fitzgibbon scores. The rank correlation coefficient between the two series is .4604, which is significantly different from zero at a 10 per cent level of significance for a two-tailed test. If *higher* defense expenditures had previously been expected to be associated with *lower* political level (which was one of the hypotheses implied by some of the previously quoted views), this hypothesis could now be confidently rejected on the basis of a positive coefficient of .46. Indeed, a positive coefficient as large as this provides some support for the hypothesis that defense expenditures are positively associated with the level of political development in Latin America.[29]

A similar result appears if *per capita* defense outlays are compared with the Fitzgibbon political development rankings. In this case, the rank correlation is .3967, which is significantly different from zero at a 20 per cent level, using a two-tailed test. Again, a positive coefficient of this size permits rejection of the notion that per capita defense expenditures are inversely related to political democracy; in fact, the coefficient provides support for the contention that per capita defense outlays are higher in countries with a higher political level. The positive relation between per capita expenditures and political democracy is not as surprising as it might seem, in view of the positive correlation between each of these and per capita income.[30]

DEFENSE EXPENDITURES AND
CHANGE IN POLITICAL LEVEL

Finally, defense expenditures are compared with change in relative political ranking in order to test the erosion-of-democracy hypothesis. Applying the procedure previously used in the corresponding tests re-

---

[29] If we had previously expected this hypothesis, we could now accept it at a 5 per cent level of significance, using a one-tailed test.

[30] For a discussion of the observed association between per capita income (as well as other measures of economic development) and political democracy, the standard references, previously cited in chapter two, are G. A. Almond and J. S. Coleman (eds.), *The Politics of the Developing Areas*, Princeton, Princeton University Press, 1960; Seymour Lipset, "Some Social Requisites of Democracy: Economic Development and Political Legitimacy," *American Political Science Review*, Vol. 53, No. 1, March 1959; and Everett E. Hagan, "A Framework for Analyzing Economic and Political Change," in Asher, Hagen, *et al.*, *Development of the Emerging Countries*, Washington, D. C., The Brookings Institution, 1962.

lating to military aid leads to similar results in the case of defense expenditures.[31]

Countries with relatively large defense expenditures include both countries whose political rank rose (Argentina, Mexico, Peru, and Venezuela), and those whose rank did not rise (Brazil, Chile, and Colombia).[32] Countries with relatively small defense expenditures include both countries whose political rank rose (Costa Rica and El Salvador), and those whose political rank did not rise (Bolivia, Ecuador, Guatemala, Haiti, and Honduras), although there are more in the latter category. Thus, the change in relative political standing appears to be unrelated to total annual defense expenditures as well as to military aid.

When defense expenditures are put on a per capita basis and compared with the change in relative political rank, a similar conclusion results. The distribution of countries over the two dichotomies is almost exactly balanced.[33] Change in relative political standing also appears to be unrelated to per capita defense expenditures.

CONCLUSIONS

Whether consideration is given to United States military aid programs or to domestic defense programs in Latin America, both the support-for-authoritarianism and the erosion-of-democracy hypotheses appear to be contradicted by the results summarized above. Larger military programs do not appear to be associated with more authoritarian political institutions. Nor do they appear to be associated with *movements toward* more authoritarian political institutions. Moreover, both of these statements hold true whether we consider the total quantity of military aid or defense outlays, or the per capita quantities.

Dictatorships, military and otherwise, are a frequent and disturbing

[31] Appendix Tables B-3 and B-4 show the distribution of countries according to change in relative political ranking compared to annual defense expenditures and to per capita defense expenditures.

[32] The exact probability of frequencies as evenly balanced as, or more unevenly balanced than, those in Table B-3 is 29.4 per cent, if the two sets of data were unrelated.

[33] The probability of frequencies as evenly balanced as, or more unevenly balanced than, those shown in Table B-4 is 54.5 per cent.

phenomenon in Latin America, but their occurrence and recurrence are not properly attributable simply to military aid or defense programs. Indeed, these factors do not appear to play a significant role in the process at all. Rather, the explanation lies in a complex set of influences rooted in Latin American history, social structure, and political tradition. George Blanksten has accurately described the problem:

> Involved in the problem of political instability . . . is the phenomenon of recurrent dictatorship. While the situation is continually changing, it is generally true that at any given moment at least a half-dozen Latin American countries are governed by dictatorships, normally military in orientation. The reasons for this are many and deep-seated; among them is the authoritarian political tradition the Spanish Empire imposed upon its American colonies. . . . Indeed, this tradition was so marked that many of the nineteenth-century leaders of movements for Latin American independence believed that monarchy should be retained as the newly independent states' form of government.[34]

Moreover, the occurrence of specifically military dictatorships is a more widespread, frequent, and long-standing phenomenon in most other areas of the world, outside Latin America, than is usually realized. Indeed, the Western tradition in this respect is more of an exception than a rule. The point is made in a striking form by S. E. Finer in a perceptive study of the historical reasons behind military interventions in politics. Of the fifty-one states existing in 1917, thirty-two have experienced military coups since 1917; and of the twenty-eight states created between 1917 and 1955, thirteen have had military coups.[35]

Viewing the matter in this light may not make authoritarian regimes, whether military or nonmilitary, more acceptable in American eyes. But it should make them more understandable, and it should make us more skeptical of easy explanations or quick solutions—in

---

[34] George Blanksten, "Fidel Castro and Latin America," in Morton A. Kaplan (ed.), *The Revolution in World Politics*, New York, John Wiley & Sons, Inc., 1962, pp. 115–116.

[35] S. E. Finer, *The Man on Horseback: The Role of the Military in Politics*, New York, Frederick A. Praeger, Inc., 1962, p. 3. Of course, these figures obscure the equally important fact that military coups may be extremely different from one another in character, motivation, duration, and effects. In one context, the "man on horseback" may be a modernizing, reforming, even liberalizing influence; in another, he may be a reactionary and repressive traditionalist.

particular, of explanations that stress military aid or defense programs, or solutions based on reductions of these programs, as a contribution to discouraging such regimes. Of course, the fact that military programs do not appear to contribute to dictatorships certainly does not provide a justification for these programs. Justification must depend on other considerations, and be judged on their merits.

Returning to the statistical tests, it should be noted, finally, that the only significant results emerging from these tests provide mild support for the notion that there may be a *positive* relationship between the level of democracy and either total or per capita domestic defense programs.[36] A rationale for this unexpected relationship is beyond the scope of this discussion, but one plausible explanation is that both per capita defense outlays and level of democracy may be positively correlated with per capita income in Latin America.[37]

In conclusion, uncertainties concerning the data that have been used should be reemphasized. The Fitzgibbon measures of political development deal in an admittedly imprecise way with some of the most complex sorts of intercountry comparisons—an always difficult and hazardous exercise. The ambiguity of some criteria, the possible irrelevance of others, and the subjectivity of the responses warrant considerable caution and tentativeness in interpreting the results. The comparisons of defense budgets that have been made also must be treated with reservations because of the problems associated with such international comparisons. Conclusions drawn from such data warrant a healthy dose of skepticism. Lest the reader move too far in this direction, however, he should ask himself what his reaction to the data would have been had the results seemed to confirm his preconceptions. At the least, the previous discussion suggests that simple and easy assertions about the political effects of military programs should be discouraged. Closer study, better observations, and more understanding are needed before accurate and useful generalizations can be made.

---

[36] Although it should be recalled that the tests performed with the defense budget data warrant special reservations, because unavailability of data made it necessary to drop five countries from the tests.

[37] For this reason, it might be interesting to compare the Fitzgibbon data with defense outlays as a percentage of gross national product (or, what is the same thing, per capita defense outlays as a percentage of per capita GNP).

Economic Programs and Political Effects: Some Indications from Latin America

Chapter Two briefly discussed several possible relationships between economic development and political development, citing various statements by government officials, historians, and social scientists. The discussion also considered evidence that has been invoked in support of these views: evidence from past revolutionary movements, from the experience of the last two decades in India and China, and from studies of economic and political data concerning the less-developed countries. These views, and the evidence adduced in their support, often differed markedly from one another. Some stressed the long-run connection between higher levels of economic development and more open, democratic political systems. Others emphasized the relationship between sustained economic growth and the survival of new democratic societies. And still other views linked economic development with the intensification of revolutionary pressures, especially in societies with major remnants of traditional status and privilege—which includes virtually all the less-developed countries of the third world. In the Marxist view, revolutionary pressures are intensified by economic development in backward countries, as well as in modernized, capitalist democracies. If it is assumed that communist leadership and control of revolutionary forces is a clear and present threat, a sequential link between economic development, revolution, and authoritarianism becomes entirely plausible.

It is not surprising that there is a wide range of views on such interactions for the issues are complex and the plausible possibilities are numerous. Simple and uniform relationships are unlikely because there are so many competing influences which may have varying weights attached to them in particular countries and time periods. Consider the following concurrent tendencies:

1. Economic development and modernization have the effect of breaking down traditional restraints and intensifying social pressures that were previously held in check. Revolution may result in the short run, but stable pluralism and decentralization may be a later outcome.

2. Economic development can create new links and points of contact in society. These linkages, and the hopefully larger pie to be divided, may open new possibilities for resolving conflicts without undue violence or authoritarianism. Economic development also provides new instruments of control that may help resolve conflicts and prevent them from getting out of hand. However, these same instruments can be used to achieve coercive centralization of power.

3. The process of development is likely to change the economic and political power of different groups. Some groups will acquire more of a stake in the existing system; other groups, less. The deprived groups may generate a coalition of the radical right or left, and in some cases of both, leading first to revolution and then to authoritarianism. On the other hand, the groups that gain may become sufficiently convinced of the opportunities for successfully "contriving reform," that radical movements are deprived of effective leadership and prospects for pluralistic political development and "reform-mongering," as Albert Hirschman has put it, may be improved.[1]

4. Development can change the aspirations level and the standard of what is considered tolerable. It can whet appetites for change and improvement by making what was formerly considered to be unattain-

---

[1] Albert O. Hirschman, *Journeys Toward Progress*, New York, Twentieth Century Fund, 1963, pp. 251–276.

able now appear within reach. The unrealism of such aspirations may be a powerful source of subsequent discontent and instability. On the other hand, development may contribute to stability by helping to bridge the gap between what is considered to be tolerable and what has actually been experienced. As a result, satisfactions may rise and social cohesion may be strengthened.

From these competing influences, many different relationships between economic and political factors may emerge in particular circumstances. It would be gratifying if we could make generalizations and predictions by testing all the possible relationships against available data and experience. But the status of our knowledge and data precludes this; many of the views and relationships that have been described earlier are more complex than can be tested using the available data. However, this chapter will try to move a little of the way toward generalizations. We shall use methods and data similar to those that were applied in Chapter Five to test a number of possible relationships between economic variables and political development.

THE DATA FOR LATIN AMERICA

As in Chapter Five, the tests that are discussed below are confined to Latin America because of the availability for that region of the Fitzgibbon data on political development over the 1950–1960 decade. The data summarized in Table 5-1 on pages 100-101, on level of political democracy and changes in political level relative to the other Latin American countries, will also be used in this chapter.[2] The methods used in this chapter to test various relationships between economic indicators and political development are the same as those previously employed to test relationships between military programs and political development. The statistical tests that will be discussed consist of comparing the Fitzgibbon political indicators with data on United States economic aid programs, and with data on gross national product, GNP per capita, rates of growth in GNP, and gross investment for the Latin American countries.

[2] See the discussion of these data above pp. 97–99. Appendix A briefly describes a variance test performed on the Fitzgibbon data that strongly confirms the nonrandom character of the respondent scores.

Some of the previously cited views implicitly or explicitly suggest that significant relationships should be expected between the economic data and the political development indicators. The purpose of the tests is to see whether these or other relationships appear to be consistent with the data. It should be noted, however, that the period covered by both the political and the economic data is short relative to the period that may be appropriate in many of the hypothetical relationships discussed in chapter two.

For comparison with the political rankings and the political-change groupings, nine separate sets of economic data for the Latin American countries will be used: (1) average annual gross national product for the 1950–1960 period; (2) gross national product per capita; (3) gross investment; (4) gross investment per capita; (5) gross investment as a percentage of GNP; (6) GNP growth rate; (7) per capita GNP growth rate; (8) total United States economic aid; and (9) total United States economic aid per capita.[3] These data are summarized in Table 6-1.

TESTING POLITICAL AND ECONOMIC INTERACTIONS WITH DATA FOR LATIN AMERICA

POLITICAL LEVEL AND ECONOMIC CONDITIONS

The first set of tests consists of comparing the ranking of the Latin American countries according to their average *level* of political development over the 1950–1960 period, as indicated in column 8 of Table 5-1, with the separate ranking of countries according to each of the

---

[3] The first seven indicators represent annual averages for the 1950–1960 period, derived principally from the U.N. *Yearbook of National Accounts Statistics, 1961.* Population figures were taken from the U.N. *Demographic Yearbook, 1962.* Data in local currencies were converted to 1960 dollar prices by using a wholesale or general price index for each country based on 1960 as the deflator and converting to dollars at 1960 official exchange rates. Growth rates for GNP and per capita GNP are compounded rates of growth, calculated from the arithmetic average of the first two years and the last two years. The United States economic aid figures represent the average annual amount of total United States aid for the 1950–1960 period, with "aid" defined to include expenditures on technical assistance, development loans and grants, Public Law 480, and disbursements under Export-Import Bank loans.

TABLE 6-1 *Selected Economic Data for Latin America*
(average annual figures for 1950–1960 in 1960 U.S. dollars except as otherwise shown)

COUNTRY	GNP (MILLIONS)	GNP PER CAPITA	GROSS INVESTMENT (MILLIONS)	GROSS INVESTMENT PER CAPITA	GROSS INVESTMENT AS PERCENTAGE OF GNP	GNP GROWTH RATE[a] (PER CENT)	PER CAPITA GNP GROWTH RATE[b] (PER CENT)	TOTAL U.S. ECONOMIC AID (MILLIONS)	TOTAL AID PER CAPITA
Argentina	9,104	466.14	1,793	91.78	19.6	2.7	0.8	332	17.36
Bolivia	274	86.57	40	12.63	14.6	-0.02	-1.4	167	51.47
Brazil	9,814	168.48	1,821	30.58	17.8	5.4	3.0	1,081	18.50
Chile	3,675	539.73	362	53.24	9.9	3.9	1.5	252	37.29
Colombia	3,277	250.35	608	46.20	18.5	2.3	0.05	283	22.34
Costa Rica	303	309.77	61	61.95	19.9	8.1	4.1	23	24.56
Cuba	—	—	—	—	—	—	—	—	—
Dominican Republic	521	207.04	91	35.90	17.2	6.7	3.1	2	0.81
Ecuador	621	161.71	94	24.46	15.0	6.0	2.9	54	14.61
San Salvador	504	199.60						8	3.46
Guatemala	529	156.93	63	18.61	11.9	5.4	2.4	63	19.38
Haiti	320	97.99	26	8.10	8.3			61	18.53
Honduras	312	186.20	45	28.07	15.2	4.6	1.4	17	10.46
Mexico	8,195	272.29	1,452	46.84	16.7	5.6	2.7	341	11.51
Nicaragua	311	229.05				3.2	-0.2	9	7.23
Panama	344	363.26	47	49.39	13.5	5.4	2.4	23	24.93
Paraguay	215	129.18				-2.3	-4.8	27	17.47
Peru	1,791	190.43	450	47.87	25.1	2.6	0.3	242	25.71
Uruguay								47	18.12
Venezuela	5,230	885.75	1,688	278.21	29.2	8.9	5.8	23	3.91

Sources: United Nations, *Yearbook of National Accounts Statistics, 1957–1961*, New York; United Nations, *Demographic Yearbook, 1962*, New York; International Cooperation Administration, *Operations Report*, June 30, 1961; Export-Import Bank, *Semiannual and Annual Reports*, Washington, D.C., 1950–1960.

Notes
a Although these investment rates are abnormally high, it should be remembered that they represent *total* capital formation, not do-
mestic saving. No adjustment has been made to subtract this surplus from gross investment to determine domestic savings. Needless to say, domestic savings rates are substantially lower.

b It is evident that several of these figures are probably too high to be accurate, for example, those for Venezuela and Costa Rica. However, in the statistical tests using these data, the growth rate figures provide a basis for (a) ranking countries and (b) grouping them in terms of whether the growth rate is or is not above the median. For these two purposes it seems unlikely that adjustment of the high growth rate figures would have much effect on the relative standing nine economic indicators. Rank correlations are computed for each of the nine comparisons, and tested for significance.[4] Table 6-2 shows the rank correlation coefficients and the significance levels for the nine correlations between the Fitzgibbon measures of political level and the separate economic data.

A few major points concerning these rough statistical tests should be noted. Consider the items of Table 6-2 consecutively:

1. The significantly positive relation between GNP and the Fitz-gibbon political ranking arises principally because the larger countries in Latin America (Brazil, Mexico, Argentina, Chile) ranked relatively high in political development, whereas the countries that ranked lowest in the Fitzgibbon scores are relatively small (Haiti, Dominican Republic, Nicaragua).

TABLE 6-2　*Level of Political Development and Selected Economic Indicators, 1950–1960—Rank Correlation Coefficients and Significance Levels*

POLITICAL LEVEL PAIRED WITH:[a]	CORRELATION COEFFICIENT	SIGNIFICANCE LEVEL[b]
1. GNP	.5939	.02
2. GNP per capita	.5774	.02
3. Gross investment	.5402	.05
4. Gross investment per capita	.5455	.05
5. Gross investment as percentage of GNP	.2455	Not significant (> .25)
6. GNP growth rate	.3272	Not significant (> .20)
7. Per capita GNP growth rate	.4478	.10
8. Total U.S. economic aid	.4696	.05
9. Total U.S. economic aid per capita	.2380	Not significant (> .25)

Source: Tables 5-1 and 6-1.

Notes

[a] The numbers of countries included in the correlations varied from 15 to 20, depending on availability of the economic data.

[b] Significance levels shown are for a two-tailed test. For a one-tailed test, based on an alternative hypothesis that specifies the sign of the correlation coefficient, the significance level in each case would be one-half that shown in the column.

[4] Cf. above, Chapter Five, pp. 99, 102–103.

2. The significantly positive correlation between per capita GNP and political development level provides support for the previously cited view that there is a positive correlation between level of economic development and level of political development.[5]

3. In intercountry comparisons, gross investment is closely associated with GNP. Hence, the significantly positive correlation between gross investment and political development level warrants the same interpretation as that associated with the correlation between GNP and political level in (1) above.

4. Similarly, the significantly positive relation between gross investment per capita and political level is closely connected to the relationship between per capita GNP and political level referred to in (2) above, and warrants the same interpretation.[6]

5, 6. Neither the ratio between investment and GNP, nor the GNP growth rate, is significantly correlated with political level. In both cases, the null hypothesis, that there is *no* relationship between the paired variables, cannot be rejected. One possible interpretation of these results is that democratic countries may exhibit slower growth rates and lower investment proportions precisely because the personal preferences of the public favor *present* over *future* consumption, and these preferences are reflected in the development decisions that are made. In the more authoritarian countries, growth rates and investment rates are more likely to reflect the "pro-growth" preferences of

[5] See above, Chapter Two, pp. 25–28.

[6] For comparison with the rank correlation coefficients, separate linear regressions were calculated of the absolute Fitzgibbon scores on per capita GNP, and of the political scores on per capita investment. If absolute magnitudes, rather than ranks, are used for both variables, quite different results are produced. For the per capita GNP regression, the linear correlation coefficient (.3623) is significant at a 10 per cent level for a one-tailed t-test, compared with the 1 per cent significance of the corresponding rank coefficient shown in Table 6-2. In the case of the per capita investment regression, the linear correlation coefficient is only .0941. This difference in results is not as surprising as it might appear, and can be fully explained by the large impact of Venezuela on the linear regressions. As shown in Table 6-1, per capita investment is three times as large in Venezuela as in the next largest country, and per capita GNP is almost twice as large, although Venezuela's political score over the 1950–1960 period was only moderately high. When Venezuela is left out of the regressions, the linear correlation coefficients are .6469 for the per capita GNP regression, and .5976 for the per capita investment regression, both significantly greater than zero at a 1 per cent level for a one-tailed t-test.

central planners rather than the "pro-consumption" preferences of the public.

7. However, rate of growth in *per capita* GNP is mildly correlated with political level. Although GNP and per capita GNP growth rates are highly correlated with each other,[7] there are a few divergences for particular countries that result in per capita GNP growth rate being more closely associated with political level than is GNP growth rate. Population growth is rapid in all of Latin America, but in some countries with a relatively high political level (for example, Brazil) population growth appears to be relatively low, whereas in countries with relatively low political level (for example, Nicaragua), population growth is relatively high. The result is to make the connection between per capita GNP growth rates and political level closer than that between GNP growth rates and political level. Some of the democratic countries may show a stronger tendency to prefer present over future consumption, and hence have lower GNP growth rates; but they may also show a slightly stronger tendency to limit their population growth than do the more authoritarian political systems, and hence have higher *per capita* GNP growth rates.

8. The significantly positive correlation between total economic aid and political level would seem to be simply another aspect of the interpretation mentioned in (1) above. Larger countries may get more economic aid because their economies and needs are absolutely larger; in Latin America, large countries rank relatively high in political development level, and small countries relatively low. There are important exceptions, of course, as in the cases of Uruguay and Costa Rica.

9. It is interesting that there is not a significant relationship between per capita economic aid and political level. The null hypothesis that there is no relationship between the two variables cannot be rejected. Some of the criticisms directed against United States aid to Latin America have suggested that the aid policy was especially associated with support for authoritarian regimes. According to this view, a *negative* correlation between economic aid per capita and level of

---

[7] The rank correlation coefficient between GNP growth rate and per capita GNP growth rate is .9625.

political development might have been expected. The results shown in Table 6-2 provide no support for this hypothesis.[8]

As mentioned in (1), (3), and (8) above, there appears to be a significant relationship between economic size and political level in Latin America, although there are important exceptions. It is interesting to note that a size ranking according to either geographic area or population is also significantly associated with political development, although the level of significance is lower.[9] It is plausible to infer from this evidence that the imposition and maintenance of political controls and restrictions may be facilitated by economic, geographic, and demographic compactness. Conversely, large size may make it more difficult to establish and maintain such controls. However, the exceptions to this generalization, both inside and outside Latin America, are sufficiently important and numerous to suggest that the relationship has only limited strength.

POLITICAL CHANGE AND ECONOMIC CONDITIONS

The second set of statistical tests is concerned with the relationship between political *change* and each of the nine economic variables. We shall again use the data from column 9 of Table 5-1[10] to establish a dichotomous grouping of countries in terms of whether their political-development rank did or did not rise relative to that of other countries. A rise in a country's rank between 1950 and 1960 indicates that the country improved its democratic standing relative to the other Latin American countries. This dichotomy in political change is then compared with separate dichotomous groupings for the nine economic variables. The groupings within the nine variables are determined by whether the observation for a particular country over the

---

[8] As discussed in Chapter Five, a similar criticism, suggesting that United States aid in Latin America has been especially directed to support authoritarian regimes, has been leveled even more strongly against military aid programs. The corresponding evidence in the case of military aid does not provide any support for this hypothesis, either. See chapter five, pp. 99, 102.

[9] The correlation coefficients in these two cases are .45 for geographic size and .39 for population size, both significant at a 5 per cent level for a one-tailed test.

[10] See above, pp. 100–101.

1950-1960 period did or did not exceed the median observation for all of the included countries.[11]

As an example of the dichotomous grouping procedure, we can consider the comparison between countries grouped according to change in political ranking, and according to per capita GNP. If a positive relationship existed between political change and per capita GNP, the countries whose relative political level rose would consist mainly of countries whose per capita GNP was *above* the median; and countries whose political rank did not rise would consist mainly of countries whose per capita GNP was *below* the median. If there were no significant relationship between political change and per capita GNP, countries whose relative political level rose would include about an even number of those with high per capita GNP and those with low per capita GNP; and countries whose political level did not rise would also include some with high and some with low per capita GNP.

The actual distribution of countries, shown in Appendix Table C-1, suggests that there is *no* significant relationship between per capita GNP and political change.[12] Of the countries that rose in political rank, five had per capita GNP above the median (Argentina, Costa Rica, Dominican Republic, Mexico, and Venezuela), and three had per capita GNP at or below the median (Bolivia, El Salvador, and Peru). Of the countries that did not rise in political rank, four were above the median per capita GNP (Chile, Colombia, Nicaragua, and Panama), and six were at or below the median (Brazil, Ecuador, Guatemala, Haiti, Honduras, and Paraguay).

For the comparisons between political change and six of the eight other economic variables, the distribution of frequencies again suggests that no significant relationship exists. Using the Fisher test, none of the relationships between political change and average annual

[11] As an additional test, separate linear regressions were also computed expressing the *change* in the Fitzgibbon scores as a function of GNP growth rates, and of per capita GNP growth rates. See below, footnote 16.

[12] According to the Fisher test, the exact probability of a distribution as even as or more uneven than shown in Appendix Table C-1 is 42 per cent, using a one-tailed test. The null hypothesis, that there is no relationship between the two variables, cannot be rejected; while the alternative hypothesis, that there is a positive relationship, can be rejected with high confidence.

GNP, gross investment, GNP growth rate, per capita GNP growth rate, total United States economic aid, and total United States economic aid per capita, is significant. In each of these six cases the hypothesis that specifies a relationship can be rejected with high confidence.[13]

In only two cases, gross investment as a percentage of GNP and gross investment per capita, does a significant relationship appear. The distribution of countries for these two cases is shown in Appendix Tables C-2 and C-3. The probability of obtaining a distribution of frequencies as even as or more uneven than those shown in Tables C-2 or C-3 is in both cases less than 10 per cent. Thus, the null hypotheses can be rejected and the hypotheses that specify a positive relationship between the gross investment proportion and political change on the one hand, and between per capita investment and political change on the other, can be accepted at a 10 per cent level of significance.[14]

This result is interesting, but not perhaps strong enough to warrant much confidence. Although an association between two variables does not imply a causal connection between them, it is nevertheless interesting to speculate on the possible interactions that may be at work in these two cases. One explanation proceeds from investment to political change, suggesting that high investment—both per capita and as a proportion of GNP—is a necessary condition for successful economic development, modernization, and for a "take-off" into self-sustaining growth. As these conditions for successful modernization are established, as evidenced by high annual average investment proportions and per capita investment, political authorities can perhaps proceed more safely to relax some controls, to widen public participation in political processes, and generally to permit institutions to change in a more democratic direction. Hence, the relationship that was found might be anticipated.

[13] In each case, the probability of obtaining frequency distributions as even as or more uneven than the observed distributions is greater than 30 per cent.

[14] Using a one-tailed test. It is perhaps worth noting that three of the countries (Bolivia, Costa Rica, and the Dominican Republic) rose in political rank by only one place. If, because of the crudeness of the measure of political change, it were considered that these countries did *not* improve in relative political performance, the amended results would *raise* the significance of the results in Table C-3 and *lower* those of Table C-2.

An alternative explanation reverses the causal chain, suggesting that political change stimulates investment. According to this explanation, political controls are likely to relax under a leadership confident that its society is stable enough to absorb freedom and that present relaxation will enhance future stability. Under these conditions, private investment is also likely to rise in response to the prevailing sense of confidence and order; and so is public investment as the leadership reallocates resources formerly needed for military and police uses. According to this view, stability and order are essential conditions for political liberalization as well as for economic growth.

Neither explanation seems powerful in the light of the preceding analysis, although perhaps the second explanation, which proceeds from political change to investment consequences, is more plausible. The first explanation suggests that investment activity may encourage political change by first affecting economic growth. However, as previously noted, there does not appear to be a significant relationship between GNP growth rates and political change in Latin America during the 1950–1960 period.[15]

As an additional test of the relationship between political change and economic development, separate linear regressions were computed expressing the change in Fitzgibbon's democratization scores as a function of GNP growth rates, and of per capita GNP growth rates. The correlation coefficients were .08 and .17 respectively, neither of which is significantly different from zero.[16] According to this test as well, there is no apparent relationship between political change and economic growth.

[15] It is interesting in this connection that a rank correlation between the Latin American countries according to GNP growth rate and gross investment proportion is *not* significant. Apparently, countries with high investment proportions are not efficient investors in Latin America; their marginal capital-output ratios evidently are relatively high. Another possible inference is that there may simply be a lag between the observation of high investment rates and the subsequent realization of higher growth rates.

[16] Denoting the 1950–1960 change in political score by P, annual growth rate by g, and annual per capita growth rate by g', the regression equations, with N=16, are:

$$P = 1.4g + 15.9, \quad \text{and} \tag{1}$$
$$P = 3.9g' + 15.8. \tag{2}$$

Standard errors of the regression estimates are 54.6 and 53.9 respectively, compared with an average value for the change in political score, P, of 21.7.

CONCLUSIONS

Notwithstanding the many reservations that should be attached to Fitzgibbon's data, the tests described in Appendix A indicate that the data do provide statistically meaningful information on the level of democracy over the 1950–1960 period. A comparison of the political level of the Latin American countries according to these data with a number of economic variables indicates there is a significantly positive relation between economic indicators of the *size* of Latin American economies and their level of political development. Thus, both GNP and gross investment are significantly associated with political level. The relationship arises principally from the fact that the larger countries in Latin America also rank relatively high in political democracy (Brazil, Mexico, Argentina, and Chile), whereas the countries that rank lowest in Fitzgibbon's scores are relatively small (Haiti, Dominican Republic, and Nicaragua). Apparently for the same reason, total United States economic aid is significantly correlated with political level as well. It is of interest to note that other dimensions of a country's "size," such as geographic area and population, are also significantly correlated with political level. The combined evidence warrants the inference that economic, territorial, and demographic compactness may facilitate the imposition and maintenance of political controls, whereas large size may make them somewhat more difficult.

Of perhaps greater interest is the significantly positive correlation between *per capita* GNP and the level of political development, as well as between *per capita* gross investment and political level. Both relationships provide further support for the conclusion reached by other studies that there is, in the long run, a positive correlation between level of economic development and level of political development.

However, the rate of growth in GNP is *not* significantly correlated with political level, nor is the ratio between gross investment and GNP significantly associated with political level. Higher growth rates and higher investment proportions do not seem to be significantly associated with higher levels of political development. One possible interpretation of these results is that democratic countries may have lower growth rates and smaller investment proportions because decisions on development policy in these countries reflect the "pro-consumption" preferences of the public rather than the "pro-growth" preferences of central planners. However, rate of growth in *per capita* GNP *is* significantly correlated with political level, though just barely so. The divergence between the results obtained with GNP growth as against per capita GNP growth rates arises because a few countries with relatively high political level (for example, Brazil and Chile) have relatively low population growth rates, whereas in other countries with relatively low political level (for example, Nicaragua), population growth is relatively high. The effect is to make the correlation between political level and *per capita* GNP growth closer than that between political level and GNP growth.

It is also interesting that there does not appear to be a significant relationship between per capita economic aid and political level. Indeed, some of the criticisms that have on occasion been directed against United States aid to Latin America have seemed to suggest that the United States gave particular support for authoritarian regimes and for restrictive political systems. According to this view, a negative correlation might be expected between economic aid per capita and level of political development. Since no such relationship appears, this criticism seems unwarranted. Distinctions between democratic and authoritarian regimes do not appear to have affected aid allocations. The argument that such a distinction *should* be made, and aid allocations adjusted in favor of more democratic regimes, is obviously not answered by the data and tests described.

The second set of statistical tests performed in this chapter was concerned with the relationship between political change and each of the nine economic variables previously mentioned. In seven of the nine comparisons, no significant relationship appears to exist. Thus, an increase in the relative degree of political democracy, as evidenced by a rise in the rank of a country in comparison with its Latin American neighbors, does not appear to be associated with GNP, per capita GNP, rate of growth in GNP or in per capita GNP, gross investment, total United States economic aid, or United States economic aid per capita. Hypotheses suggesting that higher growth rates lead to relatively higher political levels, for example, are not supported by these results. (A similar conclusion results if growth rates are compared with changes in the absolute rather than in the relative degree of democracy, as reflected by the Fitzgibbon scores.)

In only two cases does a significant relationship appear: gross investment as a percentage of GNP, and gross investment per capita. Each appears to be significantly associated with relative rise in political level. In both cases, the level of significance is 10 per cent, which does not warrant much confidence. Nevertheless, if these two significant results were accepted, how might they be interpreted? One interpretation proceeds from the influence of investment on political change; another interpretation views the process just the other way around. Although some plausible speculation can be advanced for either line of reasoning, it seems more plausible to argue that the connection works *from* changes in the socio-political environment (which make possible an easing of political conditions and an improvement in relative political level), *to* a high investment proportion, or high investment per capita, as the result.

Defense and Development

It is not surprising that military and paramilitary programs are often large in the less-developed countries. As was suggested in Chapter Two, effective military and police programs can play an important role in reconciling rapid economic change with a reasonable degree of political stability, or with the avoidance of the more extremist consequences of instability.[1] The judicious and effective use of force is as necessary a condition for the emergence of modern and moderate political systems as is economic and social development.

Chapter Two also considered the various ways in which defense and development programs can complement as well as conflict with one another.[2] In this chapter, after a brief consideration of the size of defense programs in the less-developed countries, we shall examine various ways in which military programs might contribute to economic development. How might military programs be modified in order to enhance developmental side effects without impairing military effectiveness?

[1] Chapter Two, pp. 36–39.
[2] Chapter Two, pp. 39–45.

THE SIZE OF DEFENSE PROGRAMS

One of the distinguishing, but often neglected, characteristics of many of the new countries is the large size and the important role of the defense establishments they maintain—usually with substantial external assistance. As Table 7-1 shows, for many of the principal new countries in Asia, the defense effort is substantial relative to national product and to the other usual measures of national economic scale (such as total government expenditures, gross investment, or public investment).

Table 7-2 shows the ratio between defense expenditures and each of the four other measures for seven countries: Burma, India, Thailand, Korea, Pakistan, Philippines, and Vietnam. The median proportion between defense and GNP for these countries during 1962 and 1963 was 2.8 per cent; between defense and government expenditures, 21.7 per cent; between defense and gross investment, 21.5 per cent; and between defense and government investment, 71.3 per cent.

In the Near East, defense expenditures are relatively even larger than in Asia. For eight countries in the Near East (Egypt, Iran, Greece, Israel, Jordan, Saudi Arabia, Lebanon, and Turkey), the median proportion between defense and GNP during 1962 and 1963 was 4.8 per cent; between defense and government expenditures, 22.9 per cent; between defense and gross investment, 26.8 per cent; and between defense and government investment, 91.4 per cent. In Latin America, defense expenditures are relatively smaller than in Asia and the Near East, but the amounts involved are still not negligible. For eighteen Latin American countries (Argentina, Bolivia, Brazil, Chile, Columbia, Costa Rica, Dominican Republic, Ecuador, El Salvador, Guatemala, Honduras, Mexico, Nicaragua, Panama, Paraguay, Peru, Uruguay, and Venezuela), the corresponding medians are 2.2 per cent for defense and GNP, 10.8 per cent for defense and government outlays, 12.0 per cent for defense and gross investment, and 46.0 per cent for defense and government investment.

The main reasons for these relatively large defense expenditures have already been mentioned in discussing the role of force in the

TABLE 7-1 *Defense Expenditures, National Product, Government Expenditures and Investment in Certain Underdeveloped Countries, 1962–1963*

(in millions of current dollars)

	GNP[a] 1962	1963	GROSS INVESTMENT (I) 1962	1963	GOVERNMENT EXPENDITURES (G) 1962	1963	GOVERNMENT INVESTMENT (Gi) 1962	1963	DEFENSE EXPENDITURES (Gd) 1962	1963
Burma	1,617	1,704	267	344	374	423	113	140	87	102
India	35,000	36,900	4,704	5,500	4,681	5,662	2,035	2,482	705	1,037
Thailand	3,000	3,130	540	560	449	525	140	143	74	77
Korea	2,326	3,070	315	577	568	596	187	201	157	157
Pakistan	8,127	8,340	947	1,183	802	1,072	327	542	228	216
Philippines	3,830	4,300	504	619	425	512	78	87	44	72
Vietnam	1,563	1,740	163	172	380	442	64	39	192	231

Source: Department of State, Agency for International Development, Division of Statistics and Reports, *Economic Data Book*, Washington, D. C., 1965.

Note

[a] The usual cautions about GNP and gross investment statistics in this area should be noted. Budgetary data are the most recently available estimates of central and state government expenditures. Dollar figures are converted at official exchange rates. No attempt has been made to correct for possible overvaluations.

TABLE 7-2   *Comparison Between Defense Expenditures, National Product, Government Expenditures and Investment, 1962–1963*

(per cent)

	G_d/GNP		G_d/G		G_d/I		G_d/G_i	
	1962	1963	1962	1963	1962	1963	1962	1963
Burma	6.0	5.8	23.3	24.1	32.6	29.7	77.0	72.9
India	2.0	2.8	15.1	18.3	15.0	18.9	34.6	41.8
Thailand	2.5	2.4	16.5	14.7	13.7	13.8	52.9	53.8
Korea	6.7	5.1	27.6	26.3	49.8	27.2	84.0	78.1
Pakistan	2.8	2.6	28.4	20.1	24.1	18.3	69.7	39.9
Philippines	1.1	1.7	10.4	14.1	8.7	11.6	56.4	82.8
Vietnam	12.3	13.3	50.5	52.3	117.8	134.3	300.0	592.3
	$\overline{X} = 4.8$		$\overline{X} = 24.4$		$\overline{X} = 36.8$		$\overline{X} - 116.9$	
	Median = 2.8		Median = 21.7		Median = 21.5		Median = 71.3	

Source: See Table 7-1.

Notes
G_d = defense expenditures.
G = government expenditures.
G_i = government investment.
I = gross investment.
$\overline{X}$ = arithmetic mean.

less-developed countries, and, in particular, the problem of insurgency. These countries face serious challenges to internal security deriving from their political, social, and economic vulnerabilities, combined with organized communist efforts to subvert them. Moreover, in many of these countries, internal security is threatened by factionalism and dissidence that have been stimulated by recent acquisition of political independence. When neighboring countries are communist, the defense requirements for internal security are increased by the external threat. Vietnam, Korea, and Laos are the most obvious examples.

Although the pervasive conflict between communist and noncommunist countries often plays a prominent role in these various pressures toward large defense budgets, sometimes this role is facilitative rather than causal. Long-standing animosities may be rejuvenated by independence from foreign rule, as in the case of Afghanistan and Pakistan, and of Cambodia's fears of both Thailand and Vietnam. In these cases, defense budgets are influenced by traditional hostilities as well as by cold war considerations or conflict among the great powers.

Thus, several factors contribute to the large defense budgets in many of the less-developed countries. How can we evaluate the political and economic significance of these military programs? Can alternative programs be designed that will yield greater military and/or nonmilitary benefits? There has been some public discussion of the political significance of the military in underdeveloped countries, with particular reference to prototypes like generals Ayub in Pakistan, Ne Win in Burma, Sarit and his successor Thanom in Thailand, and Park in Korea.[3] But little analytical attention has been given to the economic and political significance of military programs in the less-developed countries, and of United States and Soviet military assistance to these countries.[4] Similarly, insufficient attention has been

---

[3] See, for example, John J. Johnson (ed.), *The Role of the Military in Underdeveloped Countries*, Princeton, Princeton University Press, 1962; Edwin Lieuwen, *Arms and Politics in Latin America*, New York, published for the Council on Foreign Relations by Frederick A. Praeger, Inc., 1960; and Guy J. Pauker, "Southeast Asia as a Problem Area in the Next Decade," *World Politics*, Vol. 11, No. 3, April 1959, pp. 325–345.

[4] Among the relevant references are Edgar S. Furniss, Jr., *Some Perspectives on American Military Assistance*, Princeton, Center for International Studies, 1957; The President's Committee to Study the Military Assistance Program

given to the formulation and evaluation of alternative defense programs and military aid programs, to determine whether alternatives might be devised that would surpass the existing programs.

This chapter will consider some of the economic and, to a lesser extent, political side effects of military programs in the third world. In order to translate some of the general observations of earlier chapters into operationally meaningful terms, we shall describe a study that tried to determine whether alternative military programs might be designed that would be no less effective in military terms, but would be more effective in assisting the less-developed countries toward economic development and modernization.

SIMULATING THE ALTERNATIVE PROGRAMS

The study was concerned with developing a methodology, and attempting to apply it, to answer the following question: How can military assistance, as well as defense forces and budgets in the underdeveloped countries, be modified to generate substantially improved economic and political side effects, and yet yield about equivalent military effectiveness? Underlying the question was the notion that comparing and evaluating alternative military programs—both military aid programs and domestic defense programs—require a variety of performance measures, economic and political as well as military. For measuring military performance, the research team relied on war games, comparing outcomes in terms of area occupied in a stipulated time period, the time required to occupy or defend a specified area, casualties, and materiel and property damage. To measure economic performance, a comparison was made of the effects of alternative military programs on the *operating costs* of the defense establishment, on public *capital formation*, and on *skill formation* through technical training programs. Measures of political performance were more or less informed judgments and conjectures concerning the re-

---

(The Draper Committee), *Composite Report*, Vols. 1 and 2, Washington, D. C., 1959; Wolf, *Foreign Aid, op. cit.*; and Amos A. Jordan, Jr., *Foreign Aid and the Defense of Southeast Asia*, New York, Frederick A. Praeger, Inc., 1962.

actions of key political groups and of the public, in the countries under study, to various program alternatives. Here the study relied on "area experts" to assess performance—by no means a riskless procedure.

In an attempt to evaluate United States military assistance programs, the study was conducted in five separate steps:

1. Alternative programs were drawn up for spending a hypothetical four-year military aid dollar budget, the amount of the budget being roughly based on that which was current at the time (1960) the research was done in the particular underdeveloped countries for which the case studies were conducted, Vietnam and Iran.[5] The programs were designed to be of equal cost, but they were significantly different in content. Program A generally stressed fairly large, conventionally armed and trained forces, following rather closely the lines of established military aid programs and force structures in the major recipient countries. Program B consisted of smaller, more lightly armed forces, with the dollar savings resulting from these reductions used to expand internal security forces, to increase ground and air mobility, providing additional ground installations and airfields intended to facilitate effective intervention by free-world forces if this should be necessary; and, finally, to expand the technical training of military manpower.

Some of the specific changes made by Program B can be briefly summarized. In Vietnam, for example, savings from accepting reduction in army divisions were partly spent to construct several hundred miles of lateral east-west roads in order to connect such Vietnamese coastal cities as Da Nang, Hue, and Mo Duc with the Laos border and with other roads running from the Laos-Vietnam border into Saravane and Pakse in southern Laos. Several airfields in South Vietnam and in Thailand were expanded and provided with additional electronic equipment to permit effective operations by high-performance aircraft. Expansion of port facilities and river transportation in the Mekong Delta was also provided. The paramilitary civil guard was

[5] Although the Vietnamese situation changed sharply in the years following the study, the method and results retain relevance for other countries in the area, and for Vietnam in the future, as well.

enlarged, and additional ground vehicles, aerial reconnaissance, and transport aircraft were provided to support the smaller number of remaining ground divisions.

Changes made by Program B in Iran followed similar lines. Airfields were expanded and equipped to facilitate operations by high-performance aircraft. Improvements and additions were made in the southern road net connecting the head of the Persian Gulf with the natural defensive area in the Zagros Mountains, and in the road and railroad connections between the northwestern area around Tabriz and Turkey. Facilities were also expanded in some Persian Gulf ports. The remaining savings from reductions in army divisions were used to expand the paramilitary *gendarmerie*, and to provide additional aerial reconnaissance and transport.

Under the hypothetical Programs A and B, the same four-year dollar budget was, in effect, expended in different ways: for initial equipment (that is, *force improvement*), for four-year replacement, operating, and spare-parts costs (that is, *force maintenance*), for military construction, and for military training in United States technical service schools. Standard cost factors were used to determine equipment, maintenance, and training costs; and generous estimates were made for the construction costs of roads, airfields, and other infrastructures where accurate experience factors were not available.

2. The second step consisted of formulating a broad range of credible threats at differing levels of violence: a major insurrection; invasion by a small neighbor with only marginal support from a large communist power; and a large-scale invasion with overt participation by a large communist power.[6] The threats were sketched out in game scenarios that provided the game players with a set of initial conditions, as well as a plausible sequence of hypothetical events through which these conditions might have evolved.

The scenarios, which were completed in 1960 (before the drastic changes that subsequently occurred in Vietnam), projected events

[6] The country case studies were done in 1960, *before* the Viet Cong guerrilla war assumed a critical level of intensity in Vietnam. As noted above, one of the contingencies examined in Vietnam was a large-scale insurrection.

several years into the future in order to allow time for the hypothetical Programs A and B to be carried out. Although effort was devoted to making these projections sufficiently realistic to motivate the participants, "realism" was not the primary consideration in the design of scenarios. The scenarios were kept at a fairly broad level, and purposely excluded political details that were judged to be inessential to the games' purpose. Instead, the primary consideration in formulating the scenarios was to assure that they spanned a sufficiently wide spectrum of violence to test the military performance of the alternative aid programs.

3. Next, the research group, consisting of two teams of senior retired military officers, and a Control team, conducted the game operations, using the available military resources to try to achieve objectives specified in the game scenarios, which were then played in sequence. Because the free-world (Blue) team was assumed to have expended military aid dollars in differing ways in the pre-game period, Blue's order of battle and its logistic support resources were markedly different under the two programs, and these differences were made known to the opposing Red team. In formulating strategy and carrying out operations, Blue used in sequence the two different force and facilities packages represented by Programs A and B, while Red used his "best" strategy against each of the Blue alternatives.

4. In the fourth step, an evaluation was made of the military performance of the alternative packages primarily in terms of the time, area, and casualty measures described earlier. Occasionally, military performance was also evaluated in terms of the bargaining position of the respective teams when game hostilities were terminated, and in terms of the relative probability that a particular contingency (for example, an insurrection) would have broken out at all, depending on whether Program A or B had been implemented in the pre-game years. The evaluation technique used standard planning factors and simple quantitative models where they were applicable (for example, for assessing air-to-air combat, the effects of interdiction attacks, or movement of ground forces), but relied on discussion and experienced judgment where they were not. In comparison with other man-

machine simulations, this one placed heavy reliance on men rather than on machines.[7]

In conducting and evaluating the game, play was divided into phases, based on convenient blocks of time or space. Each phase was played under both hypothetical programs before either program was evaluated. This was to minimize the feedback that would have distorted the results if one program had been played and evaluated *before* the other was initiated.

It is worth noting that the evaluation was less concerned with the *absolute* outcomes (Who won, and by how much?), than with *comparative* outcomes (How did Program A perform compared with Program B?). One can have more confidence in comparative than in absolute outcomes, because mistakes in evaluating outcomes are likely to be correlated between the two programs.

5. Finally, independent of the war games, an evaluation was made of the economic and political side effects of the two different but equal-costing programs, A and B. The purpose of the economic evaluation was to provide a quantitative indication of differences between the two programs in their effects on economic development in the countries studied. The purpose of the political assessment was to get a qualitative indication of how the alternative programs might be received by key groups and individuals comprising the leadership of these countries.

In the economic comparisons, attention was focused on differences between Programs A and B in operating costs (and hence in budgetary impact), in the quantity of joint-use, civil-military capital facilities constructed during the pre-game period, and, finally, in the numbers of skilled technicians trained. These economic-performance measures are admittedly incomplete and only partly relevant. They leave aside, for example, the question of the productivity for the civilian economy of the joint-use capital facilities, and hence their effect on economic growth. Similarly, they do not include a measure of the productivity of technical training (such as the increase in expected

[7] For a discussion of gaming methodology, see M. G. Weiner, *War Gaming Methodology*, The RAND Corporation, Santa Monica, RM-2413, July 1959.

lifetime earnings resulting from the technical training in military schools), another factor of importance for economic development.[8] Exploration of these additional and more sophisticated economic performance measures would have been possible at some added cost in time and manpower. The measures that were used instead had simplicity and convenience to recommend them, and, for gross comparisons, seemed adequate.

In making political comparisons, our evaluation relied on the looser methods of political science. Drawing on the advice of specialists on Vietnam and Iran, we identified some of the more important leadership groups in these countries, and then relied on assessments by the area specialists of the likely reactions of these groups to the alternative programs.

POLITICAL, MILITARY, AND ECONOMIC COMPARISONS

What were the results of these comparisons? First, consider military performance. Between the two contrasting, but still technically tenable, programs, the differences in military effectiveness were neither large nor uniform. In the three-by-two matrix (covering each of the two programs in each of the three differing levels of violence) that summarized our military outcomes for Vietnam and Iran, one program produced somewhat better military performance in one contingency at one level of violence, whereas the other program did somewhat better in another contingency. But, more important, the magnitude of these differences was not large in any case. In the aggregate, factors that were not affected by the changes made in the program (for example, the terrain, the size of the existing road net, the distance of a major road junction from the border, the loyalty of the indigenous

[8] Measurement of the yield, in enhanced earning power, of investment in education and technical training is an analytically tractable problem that has begun to be explored empirically for the United States, but remains to be studied for the less-developed countries: cf. B. A. Weisbrod, "The Valuation of Human Capital," *Journal of Political Economy*, Vol. 64, No. 5, October 1961, pp. 425–436; and G. S. Becker, "Underinvestment in College Education," *American Economic Review Proceedings*, Vol. 50, No. 2, May 1960, pp. 346–354.

population) seemed to dominate factors that were affected by program changes (for example, the size and equipment of forces, and the types of facilities). In a sense, the factors that were not affected by program changes had a dominant and pervasive effect that made the over-all results more similar than different.

It should be emphasized that this last generalization applies only because alternatives were compared that were reasonable and technically tenable, although contrasting. This does not imply that changes in forces and facilities do not matter, but rather that, if these changes are judiciously designed, they seem to trade off against each other at fairly reasonable rates, leaving military performance somewhat better in some contingencies and somewhat worse in others, but not drastically different in any contingency. The additions made in Program B generally seemed to compensate for what was subtracted. For example, Vietnam's resistance against a hypothetical invasion across the 17th Parallel was to some extent weakened by the reduction in army ground forces under Program B. But, under the same program, the additional roads connecting Vietnam with southern Laos permitted a more rapid and effective deployment to meet and slow down that portion of the attack that came through Laos. In meeting the insurrection contingency, the same roads, as well as the additional reconnaissance, air transport, and river transport, provided South Vietnam's counter-insurgency forces with enough extra mobility to compensate for the reduction in the army's size, and to bring the insurrection under control in about the same time required under Program A.

The case study of Iran reached similar conclusions. The additional rail, road, and air transport, together with the extra aerial reconnaissance provided under Program B, resulted in more rapid suppression of an insurrection, especially in the less accessible areas outside Tabriz in the northwest, and near Shiraz and Esfahan in the Zagros Mountains. In the other military contingencies considered for Iran, performance was roughly equivalent under Programs A and B.

The military comparisons also suggested that trying to design a package of forces and facilities to meet a *range* of threats, rather than a single, most-likely threat, made considerable sense. The military posture that performed most effectively in one contingency—for example, in the major invasion—was not most effective in cases with a lower level of violence.

Furthermore, although sharp improvements in military effectiveness did not seem possible within existing budget levels, there appeared to be opportunities to realize modest improvements by some specific changes in the force-and-facilities mix in the underdeveloped countries along the communist periphery. Such changes related to internal security forces, mobility, reconnaissance, and at least some of the infrastructures that were described earlier.

What can be said about the economic and political side effects of the alternative programs? Not surprisingly, Program B (which sacrificed large ground forces in favor of smaller, more mobile, technically-trained forces with additional supporting facilities such as roads, airfields, harbors, and communications dominated Program A from an economic point of view. Operating costs, and hence budgetary requirements, were lowered, thereby freeing resources for developmental purposes—at least in principle. Contributions to "social-overhead" capital were expanded under Program B. And, finally, the output of trained manpower was increased because of the additional allowance of military aid funds for this purpose. The significance of these economic findings is enhanced by the fact that the military comparison did *not* indicate dominance for either program alternative. *In this, as in many other decision-making problems, it seems to make sense to base choice on secondary criteria when the primary criterion (in this case, military effectiveness) does not show clear dominance for a particular alternative.*

The political side effects were both less definite and less dominant than the economic side effects. In general, it seemed that a move in the direction of Program B might evoke support from some of the principal political elites and create a healthier public image of the role of the national military establishment, as well as of United States military assistance programs, than has usually existed in the past.

We should add a few general comments on the method that was developed and used in this study. Much of the work was necessarily imprecise, and the conclusions should be interpreted in this light. This was true not only of the political comparisons, but of some parts of the military simulation as well. For example, in comparing the time required, under Programs A and B, to quell the assumed insurrection, the study group combined numbers and facts with judgment and intuition: numbers and facts concerning differences between the programs in reconnaissance capabilities, in airlift, in ground mobility, and in response time; judgment and intuition concerning the effects of these differences on finding and killing guerrillas, on shutting off lines of communication, and on reducing the number of guerrilla incidents. In a problem as ill-structured as counterinsurgency operations, the game-seminar type of evaluation is useful, because it focuses on the known parameters and instrument variables, and makes explicit judgments concerning their uncertain effects. Moreover, although the unknown parameters (such as population loyalty, and the morale of Red and Blue units) may be highly important in the real world, the fact that we seek *comparative* rather than *absolute* results provides a useful hedge against mistaken assumptions about these parameters. There is then a high probability that errors arising from such mistaken assumptions will correlate positively, and hence that the *relative* differences in the performance of the programs will be less sensitive to them. For this reason, it seems to be particularly important in cases of this sort to pursue the analysis in parallel, so to speak, focusing on comparative rather than absolute results.

The type of judgment applied in this research has limitations. The most serious is its susceptibility to distortion by human errors. Another is that it is expensive, and requires a large number of experienced military and nonmilitary analysts. Consequently, it reduces the sensitivity testing that might be done (using many different assumptions about the unknown parameters) if the problem could be more extensively computerized.[9]

Probably the strongest merit of this method is that it enables the joining of military, political, and economic factors in the analysis, rather than focusing on one alone. In the analysis of major public policy questions, it is worth paying some price in imprecision to gain this benefit.

[9] As is currently being attempted in research on combat simulation at RAND and other research institutions.

RELEVANCE TO CONTEMPORARY
INTERNATIONAL AFFAIRS

The past two decades have seen the creation of three or four times as many "sovereign" nations as in any similar period in modern history. The mood accompanying their attainment of independence is complex, hard to categorize, and fluid. The notion of protest against Western influence, which is often stressed in discussions of the subject, is certainly an important part of this revolutionary outburst: protest particularly against foreign rule, privilege, and arrogance. (But it is not entirely accurate to imply that the protest is always against the West. Korea's protest against Japanese rule, privilege, and arrogance, for example, is essentially similar to that of the new Asian and African countries against their former Western rulers.)

In trying to channel the energy embodied in this *élan* of protest, the new countries are faced with a massive array of difficult and often conflicting problems, external and internal, military and nonmilitary. Many of the new countries of the free world face serious external military threats to their survival. If they concentrate on meeting and deterring this *external* threat, and allocate their resources accordingly, they may become vulnerable to internal stagnation, discontent, and eventual armed dissidence. Vietnam (in the 1960–1963 period, especially) and Korea both exemplify this vulnerability.

The internal and nonmilitary problems they face are no less, and often more, hazardous for the survival and vitality of the new countries: investment and technical shortages, lack of skilled manpower, population pressure, scarcity of natural resources, traditional and cultural inertia. If the new countries concentrate their energy and resources on these internal problems, they can become vulnerable to overt military pressure. India's weak military posture preceding the Chinese attack in October 1962 is a case in point.

And, needless to say, there are various combinations of internal and external vulnerability that can be exploited, as the precarious predicaments of both Laos and Vietnam suggest. How to maintain a balance between measures to counter external and internal threats, with a view toward survival and vitality, is a dilemma that is especially pertinent for the new countries on the Sino-Soviet periphery.

As if this dilemma were not enough, the new countries are often hindered in their attempt to reach such a balance by a residue of nationalism and emotionalism from the past. Such a legacy may make an obviously efficient technique appear to be a great national question mark, as was the case in Korea's long-delayed resumption of diplomatic and economic relations with Japan, or may make an obviously quixotic adventure seem a matter of high national priority, as was the case in Indonesia's fanfare over West Irian (Netherlands New Guinea) and Malaysia.

There is no easy formula for finding the proper balance between measures to counter internal and external vulnerabilities (or, among the internal vulnerabilities, between measures to counter internal *military* and *nonmilitary* vulnerabilities—namely, the vulnerability to armed guerrillas and the vulnerability to frustration and divisiveness). But part of the analytical technique for finding better answers, and for modifying them as the environment changes, may be indicated by the kind of multidimensional systems analysis that was applied in the military assistance evaluation study discussed above. In seeking to meet *military* vulnerabilities and threats, decisions and allocations can be improved by an explicit consideration of the differential *nonmilitary* effects of various alternatives. If this concept is applied, it then may become possible to derive substantial economic and social benefits from military aid programs, forces, and facilities—benefits that many of the countries of the third world critically need.

Economic Aid and the Evaluation
of Development Performance

The previous chapter suggested that one way of increasing the effectiveness of military programs is to take directly into account their economic and political side effects. The same military budget can often be used in alternative ways that *do not* differ significantly in their military effectiveness, but *do* differ significantly in their economic and political effects. In such cases, the effectiveness of military programs can be increased if the choice among alternatives is based on nonmilitary considerations.

In this chapter we are concerned with a similar question; namely, with how to raise the effectiveness of *economic* programs. More precisely, our concern is with the narrower, but still important, problem of how the performance of developing countries can be more accurately measured and evaluated, as a basis for devising more effective programs and improving aid allocations.

One of the sharpest criticisms directed against economic aid has been the lack of "businesslike" methods in administering it, and the apparent absence of clear and explicit criteria for allocating aid funds. By comparison with the balance-of-payments criterion used in planning and implementing the Marshall Plan, for example, or with the force goals and other military "requirements" used in planning military aid programs, the criteria applied in the allocation of foreign economic aid to the less-developed countries have often seemed loose, ambiguous, and changeable. The aim of encouraging effective performance by recipient countries has often been enunciated, without effecting aid decisions and allocations. As a result, the incentives facing recipient countries have sometimes been perverse: The less a country accomplishes by its own efforts, the more assistance it may be able to obtain.

The Foreign Assistance Act of 1962 made an important contribution to changing this situation by urging that more attention be devoted, in the administration of economic aid programs, to encouraging improved performance in the developing countries. To this end, the aid legislation stressed the desirability of formulating and applying criteria relating to self-help and social progress in the allocation of funds for economic development. In this chapter we consider one aspect of this problem; namely, how to evaluate the performance of developing countries, with a view to guiding United States aid policies and programs.

THE PROBLEM

The Foreign Assistance Act instructs the President of the United States, in providing aid for economic development, to take into account a number of criteria, including "the extent to which the recipient country is . . . demonstrating a clear determination to take effective self-help measures." The emphasis that is placed on this criterion has been made clear by numerous policy statements from the Administration as well as from Congress.

If one accepts the familiar reasons for emphasizing self-help, which will not be repeated here, the question arises of how this criterion can be applied. How can a meaningful, rigorous basis be provided for assessing the performance of recipient countries with respect to self-help? Although the problem is set forth here in the context of United States economic aid, it is obvious that other countries that give economic assistance have a similar concern.

The problem is, in part, one of defining what is meant by "self-help." But once a definition is adopted, there remains the question of how to provide a yardstick for assessing the *extent* to which self-help measures are being taken in relation to what a country might be expected to do. Clearly, political, social, and cultural conditions within a country have much to do with the opportunities and constraints affecting this assessment; for this the judgment of specialists familiar with each country is essential. The problem is how to supplement such judgments with a firmer, more objective standard. Without such a standard, it is difficult, and perhaps impossible, to raise the level of discussion and to toughen the inevitable negotiation and bargaining between donor and recipient countries over aid allocations.

It should be evident that measuring self-help is really a special example of the general problem of measuring and assessing economic performance in the developing countries; in general terms, "performance" may encompass savings, investment, growth rates, income distribution, and other dimensions of economic change and development.

A METHOD FOR ASSESSING PERFORMANCE

This chapter describes and applies a method for assessing economic performance.[1] The method proposes that assessment of a particular country's performance should be based partly on the performance of other countries that have identifiably *different* economic and social characteristics.[2]

---

[1] The study is described at greater length in Charles Wolf, Jr., *Savings and the Measurement of "Self-Help" in Developing Countries*, The RAND Corporation, Santa Monica, RM-3586-ISA, March 1963.

[2] In this respect, the approach is similar to that suggested in an earlier work by the author (Wolf, *Foreign Aid, op. cit.*, pp. 362–366), which discussed savings and productivity comparisons among countries as criteria for aid allocation; and by Clark (Paul G. Clark, *Indicators of Self-Help*, Washington, D. C., Agency for International Development, 1962), which ranked Latin American countries according to various indicators of self-help, and used the sum of these ranks as a basis for comparing relative performances. The present study has also benefited from earlier work on international savings comparisons by Kuznets (Simon Kuznets, "Quantitative Aspects of the Economic Growth of Nations, V: Capital Formation Proportions: International Comparisons for Recent Years," *Economic Development and Cultural Change*, Vol. 8, No. 4, Part 2, July 1960, pp. 1–96) and Houthakker (H. Houthakker, "An International

The method is general, but is applied here to only one possible measure of performance: gross government and private domestic savings, one of the important ingredients for sustained economic development. The method consists of establishing standards or norms for individual countries. These standards are derived from a multiple regression model that expresses a particular indicator of performance (in this case, savings) as a function of several indicators of socioeconomic structure (in this case, GNP per capita, foreign trade, and urbanization). The regression is fitted using cross-sectional data from a large number of less-developed countries. The resulting estimating equations can serve as indicators of *expected* behavior, based on the *actual* behavior of a large number of countries. A regression that provides a good explanation of intercountry variations in actual savings is treated as having normative significance for setting standards of performance for individual countries. Measures undertaken by a particular country to stimulate savings can be considered as especially effective to the extent that actual savings are significantly greater than predicted by the regression, or as ineffective to the extent that actual savings are significantly less than predicted by the regression.[3] Distinguishing between the countries that are significantly high and low savers provides an objective clue for assessing the extent to which countries are helping themselves in relation to what they ought to be capable of doing.

The method is similar to procedures that are familiar in quality control work, in which a range of acceptable errors or malfunctions is established, and a process or activity is said to be "normal" or "under control" so long as the actual errors that are observed fall within this range. The method is also similar to the psychologist's procedure for evaluating student achievement: establishing a normal or expected score on some standard test, based on independently

Comparison of Personal Savings," *Bulletin of the International Statistical Association*, Vol. 38, No. 2, 1961; and "On Some Determinants of Savings in Developed and Underdeveloped Countries," Stanford, Stanford Research Center in Economic Growth, 1962 [mimeographed]. Houthakker's papers, particularly the second, are especially relevant and useful.)

[3] "Significantly greater," or "less" implies that the savings residual is relatively large (for example, twice as large as the standard error of the regression estimate).

measured intelligence levels, and on the actual scores made by students in relation to that level. A student's achievement is then evaluated in terms of whether his actual score falls above or below the norm.[4]

The method proposes that performance norms for individual countries be based on regression relationships that pass two tests: (a) the regression relationships must seem sensible on theoretical grounds; and (b) they must prove to be good in explaining variations among countries in *actual* savings. While this proposal seems reasonable, there is nothing about it that compels acceptance. One might argue that actual savings are no more relevant to savings norms than actual conduct is to morality. It can be argued, for example, that savings norms should be based entirely on *a priori* considerations, such as the size of a country's trade balance, or how long a country has been independent or how close to the Sino-Soviet periphery it may be, regardless of whether these factors explain actual savings. In any event, the contrary assumption—that savings norms should be related to actual savings behavior—is at the root of the method employed here.[5]

This experimental method is applied to one measure of self-help, savings, but the approach is general. It should be possible to apply the method to formulating norms for other self-help measures, relating, for example, to the efficient use of resources rather than their mobilization, or to the allocation of resources for education and training, for building "human" capital rather than capital. The choice of savings as a measure of self-help is thus a matter of convenience; it is not intended to imply a capital theory of economic development.

The approach may also be applicable to formulating norms for measures of social and political progress,[6] such as land reform or the

---

[4] See David McClelland, *The Achieving Society*, Princeton, D. Van Nostrand Co., 1961, p. 80 ff. McClelland also suggests application of a similar approach to evaluating the performance of countries with respect to rates of economic growth.

[5] In this method, *ex ante* reasoning provides a guide to the selection of explanatory variables for inclusion in the models, but the savings norms depend on the relationships obtained from regressing actual savings on these variables.

[6] The Foreign Assistance Act also requires that the President shall, in providing development aid, take into account "the extent to which the recipient country is showing a responsiveness to the vital economic, political and social concerns of its people."

equity of taxation, or the widening of political participation. However, the grounds for expecting useful results in this case are weaker, because the variables are more difficult to quantify and their relationships more obscure.

For our present purpose, several regression models were developed, each of which used one of the following savings indicators as the variable to be explained: gross domestic savings, per capita savings, or savings as a percentage of GNP.[7] The regression equations then express the dependent variable as a function of four independent variables: GNP, GNP per capita, urbanization (measured alternatively in terms of urban income[8] and in terms of percentage of national population living in cities of 20,000 and above), and international trade. The reason for including each of these variables is its expected effect on government and/or private savings based on previous empirical work or on received theory. These reasons may be briefly summarized:

GNP AND GNP PER CAPITA

Gross savings, S, are by definition related to gross national product, Y, and extensive empirical work has established that the relationship is strong and usually stable. The reason for assuming that gross savings will vary with per capita GNP is also familiar. In general, average savings rates (S/Y) are usually higher in countries with high per capita incomes, and hence savings will tend to be higher. Higher per capita GNP will contribute to higher *government* savings because tax revenues will rise steeply if the tax system is progressive. Higher per capita GNP will also contribute to higher *private* savings because

---

[7] Gross domestic savings are defined here as gross investment minus the deficit on current international account, and minus transfers on current account. Current transfers are subtracted because they include government-to-government grant aid which in a few countries (such as Korea, Taiwan, India, and Greece) is large enough to bias savings estimates upward.

[8] The urban income estimate assumed that all income originating in the following industrial sectors was concentrated in urban areas: manufacturing; construction; electricity, gas and water; transportation, storage, and communication; banking, insurance, and real estate; public administration and defense; that all income originating in the agricultural sector was rural; and that income originating in housing, mining, trade, and services was divided between urban and rural areas in the same proportion as that between income from the six primarily urban sectors and the latter *plus* agricultural income.

higher per capita GNP is usually associated with a greater proportion of income in the form of profits and interest, and savings from these forms of income are relatively high.[9]

URBANIZATION

There are two principal reasons for supposing that urbanization may be a useful indicator for predicting savings. The first is apparent rather than real, and is related to the limitations of data collection in less-developed countries. In general, estimates of rural investment in these countries are misleadingly low, because such investment frequently involves local labor and materials that do not enter the market sector. Consumer-goods production that does not enter the market can often be estimated more or less accurately from known patterns of household consumption in rural areas, but rural capital formation is more difficult to estimate and generally is underestimated relative to rural income.[10] Since most savings estimates are based on estimates of investment, the less urbanization, the lower we would expect savings to be.

The second reason is concerned with "real" savings and investment in urban and rural areas. Assuming that rural and urban data were equally accurate, we would still expect that savings from given income would be greater in urban than in rural areas. Government savings should be higher because urban income tends to be more concentrated and easier to identify and, hence, taxes easier to collect.[11] Private savings might also be expected to be higher in urban areas because of greater exposure to the capital market. Thus, easier access to invest-

---

[9] Houthakker, "An International Comparison of International Savings," *op. cit.*
[10] The tendency has been noted in India, Indonesia, and other less-developed areas. See, for example, Wilfred Malenbaum, *Prospects for Indian Development*, Glencoe, Illinois, The Free Press, 1962, pp. 139–142.
[11] That tax collection in rural areas may be difficult and meager is strikingly illustrated by the report of the Indian Taxation Enquiry Commission which noted that land revenues in 1950–1951 amounted to only 1.2 per cent of the net value of agricultural output. Government of India, *Report of the Taxation Enquiry Commission, 1953–1954*, Vol. 1, New Delhi, 1955, p. 73. By 1960–1961, the figure had risen to 1.6 per cent, still well below the 4-per-cent level that prevailed before World War II. H. M. Groves and M. C. Mhadavan, "Agricultural Taxation and India's Five Year Plan," *Land Economics*, Vol. 38, No. 1, February 1962, p. 58.

ment opportunities may provide a stimulus to saving. Finally, industries that are relatively capital intensive, and industries that produce capital goods, are usually concentrated in urban areas,[12] which will tend to raise urban savings.

Some empirical studies suggest that urban savings rates do, in fact, exceed rural rates. Furthermore, private savings seem to be positively related to educational level and occupational status, and inversely related to family size, which supports the expectation of higher urban savings.[13] In the regression models, two alternative measures of urbanization are used, one relating to urban income and the other to urban population.[14]

INTERNATIONAL TRADE

The main reason for including international trade as a savings indicator relates to government savings. Because of the geographic concentration of goods exchanged in international trade, the relative ease of controlling such trade, and the relatively complete records that accompany it, income arising from foreign trade is more readily identifiable and tax collection from it is more effective than in the case of domestic transactions. It is a well-known fact that less-developed countries rely, for this reason, quite heavily on trade taxes of various sorts (import and export duties, tariffs, exchange taxes) as sources of revenue.[15] Hence, it is plausible to suppose that the larger a country's *total* trade, the greater its tax revenues, and the greater the potential for government savings. The sum of exports and imports of goods and services is therefore used as the relevant trade variable for explaining gross savings.

[12] Simon Kuznets, "Quantitative Aspects of the Economic Growth of Nations, V," *op. cit.*, p. 8.

[13] See, for example, National Council of Applied Economic Research, *Urban Income and Saving*, New Delhi, 1962, pp. 80–94.

[14] In the interests of brevity, this account concentrates principally on results obtained from the regressions using urban income.

[15] See, for example, Benjamin Higgins, *Economic Development*, New York, W. W. Norton, 1959, p. 511; Haskell P. Wald and Joseph N. Froomkin, *Agricultural Taxation and Economic Development*, Cambridge, Massachusetts, Harvard University Press, 1954, pp. 27–30 and 72–74.

THE MODELS

Several models were tested using these four independent variables to explain intercountry variations in savings. The first was a linear savings model:

$$S = a(Y^2/P) + b(Q) + c(U_y) + d(Y) + k + \mu \qquad (1)$$

in which:[16]

$$S = \text{gross savings}$$
$$Y = \text{GNP}$$
$$P = \text{population}$$
$$Q = \text{imports plus exports plus invisible}$$
$$\text{transactions on current account}$$
$$U_y = \text{urban income}$$

k is the intercept, and μ is a random disturbance.[17] The rationale for using each of the independent variables follows from the preceding discussion. Income squared per capita (Y^2/P) results from the previous observation that average savings (S/Y) may be expected to vary with per capita income (Y/P).[18]

The linear savings regression (1) is open to several statistical objections because of the large differences in scale among the countries. Because the cross-sectional data include countries of widely varying size, it is rather implausible to consider the observations that are to be drawn from populations as having the same variance. India's GNP, for example, will probably have a larger variance than Korea's. If an equal-variance assumption is not warranted, linear regression analysis is inappropriate, and the usual variance analysis may be misleading.[19]

[16] Except for P, all variables are expressed in 1960 United States dollars, converted from local currencies in current prices by the procedure described below, p. 12.

[17] The random disturbance, μ, is assumed to be normally distributed, uncorrelated with S, and to have zero mean and minimized variance, σ^2.

[18] An alternate form of (1), using (Y/P) instead of (Y^2/P), was also tested in the original study.

[19] Both the coefficient of determination (R^2) and the F-value may be large not because of the explanatory power of the regressions, but because the variance in the original observations is inflated by differences of scale. Since $R^2 = 1 -$

Expressing the variables as logarithms makes the assumption more plausible, *i.e.*, the logarithm of India's GNP may have the same variance as that for Korea, even though the corresponding GNP's do not. For this reason, the second model that was tested is a logarithmic version of (1).

$$\log S = a \log Y^2/P + b \log Q + c \log U_y + d \log Y + k + \mu. \quad (2)$$

For similar reasons, two other models were tested which adjust for differences in scale by using deflated forms of the variables in model (1), with population and GNP as the deflators. The per capita savings model is:

$$S/P = a(Y/P) + b(Q/P) + c(U_y/P) + k + \mu \quad (3)$$

and the average savings model:

$$S/Y = a(Y/P) + b(Q/Y) + c(U_y/Y) + k + \mu. \quad (4)[20]$$

Models (3) and (4) are statistically the most acceptable of the four, and only their results will be discussed below.[21]

THE DATA

To fit the regressions, the data used were principally derived from the United Nations *Yearbook of National Account Statistics, 1961* (New York, 1962), covering thirty-four less-developed countries for the period from 1955 through 1960, with some supplements to the United Nations data provided from statistics obtained from the Agency for International Development. (Hereafter, these will be referred to as the

---

$(\hat{\sigma}_s^2/\sigma_s^2)$ where $\hat{\sigma}_s^2$ is the variance of savings from the regression estimates, and σ_s^2 is the variance of savings from the mean), the value of R^2, which shows the proportion of the variance in S explained by the regressions, may be large because σ_s^2 is large, rather than because $\hat{\sigma}_s^2$ is small.

[20] It should be evident that (3) and (4) are not exactly deflated versions of (1). As between models (3) and (4), the former is preferable on statistical grounds because the population deflator, P, is not also an independent variable in the undeflated version of (3), whereas the GNP deflator Y appears in the undeflated version of (4). For a fuller discussion, see Wolf, *Savings and "Self-Help," op. cit.*, p. 12.

[21] For the complete results, see Wolf, *Savings and "Self-Help," op. cit.*

UN/AID data.)[22] The usual reservations concerning the reliability of this type of data should be kept prominently in mind. It should be evident that considerable caution is therefore warranted in interpreting the results. Table 8-1 summarizes the data that were derived from the UN/AID sources.

The thirty-four less-developed countries for which data were available from the UN/AID sources were distributed among the following regional groups:

1. Latin America (10):
   Argentina, Brazil, Chile, Colombia, Costa Rica, Ecuador, Honduras, Mexico, Panama, and Peru

2. Asia (9):
   Burma, Ceylon, India, Korea, Malaya, Pakistan, Philippines, Taiwan, and Thailand

3. Dependencies (during all or most of the 1955–1960 period) (11):
   Algeria, Barbados, British Guiana, Congo (Leopoldville), Cyprus, Jamaica, Malta, Mauritius, Nigeria, Puerto Rico, Rhodesia-Nyasaland

4. Latin America, plus Latin American dependencies (14):
   All of the Latin American countries in Group 1, plus the following four from the dependencies group: Barbados, British Guiana, Jamaica, Puerto Rico

5. Other countries (4):
   Greece, Israel, Portugal, and Sudan

The following discussion is based on the results obtained by combining all thirty-four countries (Groups 1, 2, 3 and 5).[23]

---

[22] Where population figures were needed, we relied on the United Nations *Statistical Yearbook, 1961*, New York, 1962, and the United Nations *Demographic Yearbook, 1960*, New York, 1961. For the time series data, the median value for each country was selected because the medians were considered to be a better indicator of central tendency than the means. For such a short period, the mean would be more subject than the median to distortion by unusual fluctuations over one or two years.

In processing the data, the procedure followed was to deflate the 1955–1960 time series by a general or wholesale price index for each country based on 1960 prices, and to convert to United States dollars using the 1960 exchange rates of the International Monetary Fund.

[23] Results for the regional regressions are discussed more fully in the original monograph summarizing the entire study. See footnote 1, this chapter.

TABLE 8-1   Selected National Accounts Data (UN/AID)

(median values, in millions of U.S. 1960 dollars, except as otherwise indicated)[a]

COUNTRIES	PERIOD COVERED	GROSS SAVINGS (s)	GNP (Y)	SAVINGS RATE (s/Y) (PER CENT)	PER CAPITA GNP (Y/P) (DOLLARS PER PERSON)	TOTAL EXPORTS PLUS IMPORTS (Q)	INTERNATIONAL TRADE RATIO (Q/Y) (PER CENT)	URBAN INCOME (Uy)	URBAN INCOME (Uy/Y) (PER CENT)
1. Latin America									
Argentina	1955–1960	1,696.35	9,199.50	18.4	467.35	2,094.73	22.8	6,700.14	72.8
Brazil	1955–1959	1,607.80	10,816.00	14.9	176.54	1,748.43	16.0	6,640.10	61.4
Chile	1955–1960	328.51	4,182.80	8.1	576.91	1,228.87	28.7	3,104.37	74.2
Colombia	1955–1960	643.70	3,262.70	19.0	243.95	1,111.87	32.5	1,582.49	48.5
Costa Rica	1955–1960	55.62	363.36	15.5	343.40	196.14	53.3	174.98	48.2
Ecuador	1955–1960	100.28	693.99	14.2	173.98	281.75	40.5	330.89	47.7
Honduras	1955–1959	38.27	325.73	11.6	186.00	154.07	44.4	114.45	35.1
Mexico	1955–1960	1,550.80	9,487.85	16.4	297.51	3,150.80	33.6	7,115.89	75.0
Panama	1955–1960	20.56	372.95	5.9	380.21	267.58	73.4	179.91	48.2
Peru	1955–1959	382.27	1,763.90	21.5	178.81	890.17	51.5	1,108.01	62.8
2. Asia									
Burma	1956–1960	193.49	1,133.80	15.4	56.54	486.13	45.0	472.62	41.7
Ceylon	1955–1960	118.64	1,185.35	9.8	127.22	825.51	71.5	441.36	37.2
India	1956–1959	3,188.00	31,450.00	10.2	79.34	4,319.00	14.0	10,528.58	33.5
Korea	1955–1960	70.49	1,893.40	4.6	83.72	309.73	16.0	743.77	39.3
Malaya	1956–1959	283.14	1,637.55	17.3	257.45	1,496.91	89.8	537.14	35.0
Pakistan	1955–1960	525.36	6,190.00	8.2	69.24	896.43	15.2	1,732.23	28.0
Philippines	1955–1960	267.27	3,607.20	7.4	149.97	944.80	26.5	1,732.96	48.0
Taiwan	1955–1960	139.82	1,333.05	10.8	135.07	391.30	29.3	768.04	57.6
Thailand	1955–1959	300.51	1,952.80	14.8	81.03	735.09	40.5	925.18	47.4

	Period								
3. Dependencies									
Algeria	1955–1959	151.17	2,695.90	5.6	265.79	1,486.52	60.2	1,768.81	65.6
Barbados	1954–1959	9.79	62.69	15.4	270.58	74.33	119.9	34.90	55.7
British Guiana	1955–1959	21.31	137.39	15.5	270.33	137.41	99.4	86.68	63.1
Congo (Leopoldville)	1957–1959	180.07	1,210.90	14.9	89.53	1,243.02	100.5	734.23	60.6
Cyprus	1956–1960	40.95	245.00	17.3	446.27	251.43	105.8	162.42	66.3
Jamaica	1955–1960	101.63	591.29	15.9	366.69	411.59	68.3	452.91	76.6
Malta	1955–1960	21.91	129.17	17.0	402.99	164.57	127.5	102.51	79.4
Mauritius	1955–1960	26.12	146.04	18.0	249.91	125.60	86.8	86.10	59.0
Nigeria	1953–1957	230.35	2,588.80	8.5	83.39	885.93	33.9	510.17	19.7
Puerto Rico	1955–1960	154.69	1,439.75	11.1	625.06	1,628.42	114.0	1,142.31	79.3
Rhodesia-Nyasaland	1955–1960	299.05	1,244.85	21.8	165.21	1,347.29	102.8	791.19	63.6
4. Latin America plus Latin American Dependencies[b]									
5. Other Countries									
Greece	1955–1960	320.37	2,923.65	11.0	359.40	1,026.69	34.5	1,633.43	55.9
Israel	1956–1960	277.56	2,026.90	13.7	1,014.97	836.26	41.3	1,728.37	85.3
Portugal	1955–1960	260.23	2,068.10	12.6	231.20	1,486.52	43.3	1,343.74	65.0
Sudan	1955–1960	87.54	827.64	9.3	80.64	331.39	35.6	217.57	26.3

Source: See text, pp. 145–146.

Notes

a In comparing percentage figures with the ratio between the corresponding dollar figures, it should be noted that, for example, median (S/Y) is not necessarily equal to median S/median Y; however, in most cases the difference is negligible.

b This group includes Group 1 plus the four Latin American dependencies shown in Group 3: Barbados, British Guiana, Jamaica, Puerto Rico.

STATISTICAL RESULTS

In the statistical procedure that is followed, we use the coefficient of determination, R^2, to assess the ability of each regression to explain intercountry variations in savings, and the Geary-Pearson method to test the regression residuals for normality.[24] If the hypothesis embodied in a regression is not to be rejected, the residuals (represented in the regression models by the disturbance term, μ) should be normally distributed with zero mean.

The regression coefficients resulting from the per capita savings model are shown below; standard errors are in parentheses, and the coefficients that are significantly different from zero are marked with asterisks:

$$S/P = .078^* (Y/P) + .027^* (Q/P) + .042 (U_y/P) + 3.906 \quad (3)$$
$$ (.057) (.019) (.632) (5.260)$$

R^2 is .8272 and F is significant at the .005 level adjusted for degrees of freedom. The coefficient of per capita GNP is significantly different from zero, as is that for per capita international trade. Rerunning the regression after dropping the insignificant variable (U_y/P) gives the following coefficients and standard errors:

$$S/P = .114^* (Y/P) + .029^* (Q/P) + 1.479 \quad (3.1)$$
$$ (.015) (.018) (3.563)$$

R^2 (.8249) is nearly the same as in model (3), and F is also significant at the .005 level. In addition to the significant correlation, the per capita savings model (3.1) successfully passes the test for normally distributed residuals.[25] Therefore, on the basis of both the results ob-

---

[24] R. C. Geary and E. S. Pearson, "Tests of Normality," *Biometrika* Office, University College, London, 1938, cited in Carl A. Bennett and Norman T. Franklin, *Statistical Analysis in Chemistry and the Chemical Industry*, New York, 1954, pp. 80–83 and 92–96. The Geary-Pearson method consists in deriving a measure of skewness, $G_1 = k_3/k_2^{3/2}$, and of kurtosis, $G_2 = k_4/k_2^2$, where k_2, k_3 and k_4 are the second, third and fourth semi-invariants of the regression residuals, respectively. Critical values of g_1 and g_2 are derived by Bennett and Franklin from the Geary-Pearson paper.

[25] Applying the Geary-Pearson test to the residuals of model (3.1) gives g_1 and g_2 values of $-.47$ and $.62$ [for the unreduced model (3), the corresponding values

tained for the coefficient of determination and for the normality test, the per capita savings model has considerable merit.

It is worth pointing out that using urban population (U_p) instead of urban income in (3) has the effect of making the regression coefficient for the urbanization variable significant, as well as increasing R^2 and F.

$$S/P = .057^* \, (Y/P) + .107^* \, (Q/P) + 65.222^* \, (U_p/P) - 5.460^*$$
$$\quad\quad (.027) \quad\quad\quad (.030) \quad\quad\quad (33.920) \quad\quad\quad (1.331)$$
$$(3.2)$$

R^2 is .8752 and F is significant at the .005 level. Thus, this regression gives a better explanation than (3) and (3.1), although it should be recalled that four fewer countries are included due to the limited coverage of the urban population data. In order to obtain regression estimates for all countries in the original sample, we therefore continue to use the results from model (3.1) in the later discussion.

The results from the average savings regression (4) [a deflated version of model (1) with Y as the deflator] are shown next.

$$S/Y = -.00006 \, (Y/P) + .039^* \, (Q/Y) + .123^* \, (U_y/Y) + .060$$
$$\quad\quad (.00005) \quad\quad\quad (.022) \quad\quad\quad (.063) \quad\quad\quad (.026)$$
$$(4)$$

Although the coefficients of the trade and urban income proportions are significantly different from zero, R^2 is only .2474. While the correlation is thus weak, the average saving model (4) passes the Geary-Pearson test for normally distributed residuals. However, as the small R^2 indicates, model (4) does not give a good explanation of inter-country variations in savings. Hence, (4) cannot provide a plausible standard for assessing the performance of individual countries. Such a standard is provided, however, by the per capita savings model (3.1), which was the most satisfactory of those tested.

---

are $-.41$ and $.55$]. These results are *below* the critical levels of g, and hence the hypothesis of normally distributed residuals cannot be rejected.

COUNTRY RESIDUALS AND THE PROBLEM OF ASSESSING PERFORMANCE: CONCLUSIONS AND QUALIFICATIONS

What bearing do these results have on the original problem of evaluating country performance with respect to self-help? According to the approach suggested earlier, a regression model that provides a generally good explanation of intercountry variations in savings, as reflected in a high R^2, can plausibly serve to establish norms for evaluating the actual savings of individual countries. On this basis, as we have seen, the per capita savings model is the most useful among those we have considered.

From the standpoint of the problem of self-help, it is therefore of interest to examine the individual country residuals obtained from the reduced form of the per capita savings regression (3.1). Table 8-2 shows (in Columns A, B, and C) actual and predicted per capita savings and residuals for the individual countries. Countries that are *significantly* high or low per capita savers, as indicated by residuals that are at least one standard error from the regression norm, are marked with an asterisk.

On the basis of the 1955–1960 data, five countries appear as significantly high savers (Argentina, Colombia, Peru, Jamaica, and Rhodesia-Nyasaland), and four as significantly low savers (Chile, Panama, Algeria, and Puerto Rico). These results are generally consistent with qualitative information about the savings characteristics of these countries, as well with the absolute magnitude of their average savings rates. As Table 8-1 shows,[26] Argentina, Colombia, Peru, Jamaica, and Rhodesia-Nyasaland had savings rates of 18.4 per cent, 19.0 per cent, 21.5 per cent, and 21.8 per cent, respectively, in the 1955–1960 period. For the four countries having significantly low per capita savings, according to the regression, the savings rates in Table 8-1 are Chile, 8.1 per cent; Panama, 5.9 per cent; Algeria, 5.6 per cent; and Puerto Rico, 11.1 per cent. In effect, the per capita regression model provides a loosely-grained filter that identifies nine countries

[26] Above, pp. 140–141.

TABLE 8-2 *Comparison of Actual and Predicted Savings*
(in 1960 U.S. dollars)

COUNTRIES	(A) ACTUAL PER CAPITA SAVINGS (1955–60 MEDIAN)	(B) PER CAPITA SAVINGS PREDICTED BY SAVINGS MODEL (3.1)	(C) PER CAPITA SAVINGS RESIDUAL (A − B)
1. *Latin America*			
Argentina	84.56	57.52	27.04*
Brazil	26.24	22.33	3.91
Chile	45.57	71.84	−26.28*
Colombia	46.83	31.49	15.35*
Costa Rica	52.67	45.78	6.89
Ecuador	25.14	23.25	1.89
Honduras	21.63	25.09	−3.45
Mexico	48.63	38.08	10.56
Panama	20.95	45.42	−24.46*
Peru	38.52	24.34	14.18*
2. *Asia*			
Burma	9.60	8.59	1.01
Ceylon	12.79	18.47	−5.68
India	8.07	10.80	−2.73
Korea	3.14	11.38	−8.23
Malaya	43.46	37.28	6.18
Pakistan	6.05	9.63	−3.58
Philippines	11.29	19.64	−8.35
Taiwan	14.45	17.97	−3.52
Thailand	12.84	11.58	1.27
3. *Dependencies*			
Algeria	14.90	35.84	−20.94*
Barbados	42.66	41.48	1.17
British Guiana	41.39	39.80	1.58
Congo (Leopoldville)	13.28	14.27	−0.99
Cyprus	74.58	65.24	9.34
Jamaica	63.02	50.41	12.62*
Malta	68.37	61.92	6.45
Mauritius	43.89	35.89	8.00
Nigeria	7.36	11.75	−4.39
Puerto Rico	67.17	92.67	−25.50*
Rhodesia-Nyasaland	38.94	25.25	13.69*
4. *Others*			
Greece	39.38	45.89	−6.50
Israel	138.99	128.67	10.31
Portugal	29.09	32.48	−3.39
Sudan	8.05	11.51	−3.45

Source: Table 8-1 and text.
Note: An asterisk indicates that the residual is significant in the sense that it is more or less than one standard error from the regression estimate. For the per capita savings regression (3.1), the standard error was $12.33.

as significant outliers among the thirty-four countries included in the sample.

The rough correspondence between the significant regression residuals and the average savings rates does not, however, imply that the savings rates can be used as a simple and straightforward substitute for the regression results. As Table 7-2 shows, there are other countries in the sample with savings rates as high and as low as these figures that do *not* emerge as significantly high or low *per capita* savers according to the regression analysis. Therefore, while the savings rates are useful as a check on our results, they are not a substitute.

Given the quality of the data and the well-known hazards of international comparisons, these results should be considered preliminary, and interpreted with a generous dose of caution. However, granted this basic reservation, the foregoing discussion and results are of interest in two different contexts.

First, they are of interest in connection with the general problem of savings behavior in the less-developed countries. To summarize the main findings, the savings equation that best meets the two tests that we have applied is a linear regression of per capita savings on per capita income and per capita international trade. When urban population as a proportion of total population is used as a third independent variable, its regression coefficient is also significant and the power of the regression to explain intercountry variations in per capita savings is improved.

Second, from the standpoint of formulating performance norms, the aim of the foregoing regression analysis is to provide a basis for comparing what countries are achieving, with what their economic characteristics suggest they should be capable of achieving. The significant results indicate that it is possible to give fairly rigorous meaning to the legislative mandate to consider "the extent to which recipient countries are taking effective self-help measures" in deciding on aid allocations. This is not to say that special country circumstances and other United States policy considerations are not important for aid decisions; clearly, they are. But a means of providing some objective indicators of what countries should be capable of doing for themselves can serve a useful purpose in raising the level of discussion and understanding of some of the ground rules applying to development aid programs, both in the developing countries and in the United States.

Nevertheless, a number of important cautions should be borne in mind in appraising the method and results. Reviewing and improving the sorts of data we have used would be highly desirable. For example, in at least one case, Argentina, the apparently high savings may be due more to inadequate allowance in the data for the effects of inflation than to the actual volume of real savings. From the standpoint of the performance problem, the country residuals should be regarded primarily as providing an important *clue* rather than a conclusion.

Several other limitations arise in this broader context of self-help and performance measurement. It can be argued, for example, that, from the standpoint of foreign aid allocations by donor countries, it is more important to focus on rates of *change* in savings, rather than *levels* of savings or per capita savings.[27] Moreover, the attempt to assess a country's performance with respect to savings involves, at best, only one aspect of "self-help." Although saving is an important indicator of resource mobilization, it is not necessarily the most important contributor to sustained economic development. In principle, of course, it may be possible to apply this method to the assessment of other dimensions of self-help, relating, for example, to the efficient use of resources, rather than their mobilization, or to the allocation of resources for education and training, rather than for adding to physical capital. Indeed, it may also be feasible to extend the method beyond self-help to other dimensions of country performance, such as growth rates and income distribution. But as it stands, the analysis described here is concerned with only a single dimension.

Nevertheless, the exploratory approach summarized in this chapter may be of use in decision-making. By mobilizing objective and quantitative information in a meaningful way, the method can help the

---

[27] Some preliminary statistical work, involving a regression of rates of change in savings on rates of change in the independent variables used in the present study, did not produce meaningful results. For a discussion of some of the peculiar properties associated with marginal savings regressions, see Wolf, *Savings and "Self-Help," op. cit.*, pp. 18, 37, 38.

decision-maker to take some of the dimensions of country performance explicitly into account in making decisions on aid allocation.
It can thus help in establishing some firmer rules of the foreign aid
"game" than have usually been applied, and can thereby provide a
positive incentive for the developing countries to perform effectively
in contrast to the perverse incentives that have sometimes rewarded
malperformance in the past.

Coordination Between Economic and Military Programs

Chapter Seven considered the possibility of redesigning military programs to enhance economic and political side effects without degrading military effectiveness. Chapter Eight considered one aspect of the problem of increasing the effectiveness of economic aid programs: developing improved measures of performance, in terms of which accomplishment can be assessed and aid allocations reconsidered. These discussions lead directly to the general question of whether and how coordination between economic and military programs can be improved.

Why is it important to coordinate the United States economic and military aid programs in the less-developed countries? Given the competitive and complementary relationships between military and economic aid programs that were discussed in Chapter Two, the answer is that coordination is important in order to: (1) clarify the *competitive* relationships so that, where choices have to be made between the programs, they can be made more "rationally"; and (2) profit from the *complementary* relationships so that each program can help to advance the objectives of the other program to the advantage of over-all United States interests.

Coordination is a major problem in a relatively small number of countries on the Sino-Soviet periphery for which both military and economic programs have been large: Korea, Vietnam, Thailand, India, Pakistan, Iran, and Turkey. In some other countries (for example, the Philippines, Brazil, and Ethiopia), the coordination problem exists, but it is more limited because the military programs are smaller. In the majority of African and Latin American countries that receive aid, the coordination problem is of much less significance. Nevertheless, two important points should be noted: (1) The countries in which the coordination problem is quantitatively significant, though few in number, receive a large share of total United States military and economic aid—in recent years, considerably over 60 per cent of the total; (2) Even in countries in which the problem is quantitatively small (for example, in Brazil, Chile, Colombia, Peru, and Argentina), some attention to improved coordination between programs can help to make the indigenous military establishment a more effective contributor, rather than an obstacle, to nation building. Similarly, as suggested in the discussion of insurgency in Chapter Three, improved coordination between economic and military programs is important if capabilities to counter and control insurgencies are to be strengthened.

In the following discussion, "military aid" refers to programs for which an acceptable measure of performance can be stipulated in terms of specific military outputs, such as force units, delivery capabilities, and military infrastructures. "Economic aid" refers to programs for which an acceptable measure of effectiveness can be approximated in terms of various economic and social outputs, relating, for instance, to changes in the quantity and distribution of income and wealth. This distinction is useful notwithstanding the fact that the ultimate objectives of both programs are "political," in either a short-term or long-term sense. The military or economic outputs are usually only intermediate aims, the true value of which depends on their contribution to political objectives. But the distinction remains useful because the political basis for choosing between greater or lesser emphasis on one program or another can often be clarified by explicitly identifying the intermediate outputs—military or economic—that may be gained or lost by making one or another choice. A clearer basis for choice can contribute to better decisions.

Admittedly, there is arbitrariness in placing a given amount of aid in the military or the economic aid category, and then attributing the real impact of the aid to military or to economic effects. Because resources are fungible, aid provided by the United States under one label and with one set of intended effects may lead the recipient country to make offsetting changes in the use of its own resources—either its domestic resources or foreign exchange. The actual result may thus be different from the intended result.[1]

But for many reasons, such substitutability is seldom complete. Major differences in aid *categories*, in the *form* in which aid is provided, and in the *intentions* of the United States as expressed in its informal negotiations and understandings with the recipient country, can and do permit differing end results to be achieved and identified. In some instances, the commodity form of aid (for example, military equipment or chemical fertilizers) may permit a reasonable attribution of end use to the military or economic categories. In other cases, it is often possible and helpful to use the intention of the United States in providing the aid as the criterion for making the distinction, regardless of the commodities that are provided. This point, together with its implications for program coordination, will be discussed further.

CURRENT PLANNING AND PROGRAMMING TECHNIQUES

MILITARY ASSISTANCE PROGRAM (MAP)

The planning of United States military assistance programs is based on comprehensive guidance from the Department of Defense, describing broad and specific United States policy objectives by region and by country, as well as specifying the military tasks that warrant emphasis in aid programming. Within this framework, the planning of five-year military assistance programs on a regional and country-by-country basis depends on (1) the force goals and base requirements

---

[1] For a discussion of the fungibility (substitutability) problem in foreign aid, see Wolf, *Foreign Aid, op. cit.*, Appendix I, "The Problem of Substitutability in Foreign Aid," pp. 417–419.

established by the Joint Chiefs of Staff (JCS); and (2) the approximate dollar guidelines sent by the Department of Defense, after interagency approval, to the unified commanders in the Pacific, European, and Southern (Latin American) commands.[2]

Within the regional guideline figure, the unified commander establishes dollar guidelines for each country in his command. These country guidelines are intended to help the United States Military Assistance Advisory Group (MAAG) in each country to guide the five-year planning of MAP (for example, for fiscal years 1967–1971), as well as to serve as a basis for preparing a refined program for the immediately following fiscal year (for example, FY 1967). Given the JCS force goals and base requirements, and the country dollar guidelines set by the unified commander, each MAAG prepares and submits its proposed five-year military equipment and training plan. The MAAG plans are initially submitted to the unified commander and include the *total* estimated local defense budget costs, with which the MAP dollar programs are associated. These total defense costs are broken down into the portion that is expected to be financed by the country itself, as both domestic expenditures and foreign exchange, and the portions for which foreign support is to be attributed: from United States supporting assistance funds, from funds derived from the sale of United States surplus agricultural commodities (under the Agricultural Trade and Development Act), or from assistance from other countries. The MAAG submissions also indicate what shortfalls in the JCS goals, if any, will result under the planned program, and whether these shortfalls are acceptable or unacceptable in relation to United States objectives and to anticipated threats.

The MAAG submissions are reviewed by the unified commander, who then approves, modifies, cuts, or reschedules (for example, by stretching out the MAAG delivery schedules). As finally modified and approved by the unified commander, the regional programs are submitted by him to the Department of Defense.

Submissions from the unified commanders are then reproduced and

---

[2] The dollar guidelines contain both a firm MAP figure for each region to guide preparation of a refined program for the immediately following year, and a target dollar figure for each of the next five years. For a more extensive discussion of programming and planning procedures, see Jordan, *Foreign Aid and the Defense of Southeast Asia, op. cit.*, pp. 40–70.

distributed by the Department of Defense as the basis for interagency review of the refined, operating program for the next fiscal year, and of the five-year MAP plan. The interagency review provides an opportunity to consider in Washington issues that may be raised by the submissions from the field, such as those relating to the important but often implicit political aspects of the programs, the significance of program shortfalls, and the size and sources of financing for local costs.

Following the interagency review, a submission is made to the administrator of the Agency for International Development (AID) in his role as foreign aid coordinator, and then to the Budget Bureau. The Budget Bureau submission requests an allotment and approval to implement the refined program for the current fiscal year (say, 1967), as well as approval of the basic estimates underlying the five-year plan as a basis for congressional presentation. After action by the Budget Bureau, and Defense Department consultation with the unified commanders and the MAAGs, program revisions are made so that the Operating Year Program can be approved for execution and congressional presentation of the next year's program (for 1968) can be completed.

ECONOMIC AID

Until recently, the planning of economic aid has taken place largely on an annual basis. On the basis of very broad and general United States policy objectives, AID missions have established goals for particular economic sectors and identified project priorities within each sector. Based on broad judgments concerning "absorptive" capacity (how much aid a particular country can "productively" use) and the availability of aid funds, country programs have been recommended by the AID missions as a mixture of projects from different sectors. The resulting programs have included some indication of the way these projects are expected to contribute to the sectoral goals, but they usually have included little or nothing on how the sectoral goals related to national objectives of the country itself, or to United States objectives in the country. AID planning has thus lacked a counterpart to the JCS force goals for MAP.

Since 1963, AID has been shifting country planning to a five-year basis, and relating United States aid to the attainment of specific objectives. It is intended that these objectives be specified with sufficient precision to permit measurement of progress as well as assessment of the consequences of possible shortfalls. The aim is to produce a Long-Range Assistance Strategy (LAS) for countries that receive a major amount of aid. These modifications in AID planning have been tested and refined in several countries, and on the basis of these tests, the LAS is being further adapted for more general use.[3]

In drawing up the LAS, AID missions are asked to estimate an "optimum" level of United States assistance, recommending the aid level necessary to meet United States goals, specified in economic, social, and political terms, for the country concerned. The LAS is to be formulated on the assumption that this optimum level of assistance will be available over the five-year period.

As part of the LAS, attention is being focused on specific programs and measures for increasing the mobilization of resources for economic development within recipient countries and assuring their more efficient use, as well as for providing for increased social equity, opportunity, and mobility. Such measures of self-help and social progress are intended to be assessed as precisely and quantitatively as possible, to permit comparisons to be made among countries and to help identify bottlenecks within countries.[4] This assessment, supplemented by nonquantitative judgments, will help AID to make better allocative decisions, and AID missions in the field to improve program formulation.

IMPROVING PROGRAM COORDINATION

The aim of improving coordination between economic and military aid programs is to increase the contribution they make to furthering over-all United States objectives in recipient countries. In general terms, the following steps would facilitate coordination:

[3] For a more detailed discussion of the new approach to planning economic assistance, see United States Agency for International Development, Program Coordination Staff, *Principles of Foreign Economic Assistance*, Washington, D. C., 1963.

[4] For a discussion of one method of making meaningful comparisons among countries in terms of the degree of self-help they are demonstrating, see Chapter Eight above.

(1) United States objectives would be formulated in terms that have operational meaning for economic and military programs; (2) Planning and administration of each program would include a deliberate effort to understand and advance the objectives of the other program, insofar as this can be done without consequential cost to the cooperating program; and (3) Where conflicts arise between military and economic programs (as indeed they must if only because of competition for scarce United States and local resources), AID, the Department of Defense, and their components in the country team, would conscientiously seek to clarify the issues that are involved, to provide a better basis for choice.

Such recommendations are easy to make. The difficult problem is to make changes in techniques, and in attitudes, that will in fact contribute toward improved coordination. The following discussion tries to identify some inadequacies in present methods and to suggest ways of making improvements in them.

Underlying the analysis of Chapter Seven is the premise that, in many instances, military tasks or missions can be performed in different ways. For example, in meeting or deterring external aggression, additional time can be bought by providing larger indigenous forces, or by building infrastructures and ground environment that will facilitate more rapid commitment of United States or allied forces. In different contingencies, different alternatives may be preferable. Hence, as noted in the case studies that were summarized in Chapter Seven, the military consequences of some equal-cost alternatives may not be appreciably different, although their side effects may be substantially different. In such cases, where the primary criterion relating to military effectiveness yields approximately equivalent results for several alternative programs, the choice among them should be explicitly based on secondary criteria concerning economic and social side effects.

This conclusion suggests certain ways in which military assistance programs might be better coordinated with economic programs. For instance, the five-year planning of military programs could formulate and test alternative combinations of forces, equipment, and infrastructures, within the specified country dollar guideline figures, along the lines described in Chapter Seven. The primary criterion of choice, the military effectiveness of the alternatives, could be assessed using both traditional military analysis and simulation techniques.

In addition, the effectiveness of the alternative programs should be assessed in terms of secondary criteria relating to economic and political side effects. Economic analysis should be applied to the alternative programs in an effort to compare local budgetary costs; balance-of-payments effects; impact on the supply of skilled and semiskilled manpower to the civilian economy; and impact on civilian production and investment. The aim of the comparison should be to find a combination of forces, equipment, and infrastructures that is approximately as effective in military terms, in the relevant military contingencies, as the alternative program, and yet performs substantially better in economic and political terms.

In addition to such studies, much can be done to enhance the secondary benefits derived from military programs in those underdeveloped countries whose military establishments are relatively large. In these countries the armed forces are often one of the more efficiently and honestly run institutions. It can be a powerful agent of nation building and modernization.[5] The emphasis that is already placed on civic action programs under MAP represents major progress in this direction. But there are important additional possibilities. For example, in locating new bases or other infrastructures, consideration should be given to the developmental side effects of alternative locations. MAP technical training programs can be reviewed and possibly revised to permit greater benefits to be derived from them by the civilian economy. The Table of Organization and Equipment of army divisions could be modified to increase the proportion of engineering units; and the use of such units and their related equipment for civilian construction purposes might be expanded considerably without loss of military effectiveness. In order to take advantage of the opportunities that exist, more analytical attention should be devoted to them in drawing up and presenting the annual five-year MAP plans. As a step in this direction, the MAAGs should be asked to identify and analyze the specific measures and projects by which the

[5] For a general discussion, see John J. Johnson (ed.), *The Role of the Military in Underdeveloped Countries*, Princeton, Princeton University Press, 1962.

local military establishment can provide benefits to the civilian economy, and to estimate the value of such benefits that are being or could be provided.

This approach also applies to the design of economic development programs. In some cases the sequence (or the location) of development projects can be adjusted to have beneficial effects on current military security conditions, or on military contingencies that may arise. Examples of such side effects were stressed in discussing programs for counterinsurgency in Chapter Three. Often it is also possible and desirable for the planning of economic development to take into account the numbers and types of military manpower expected to be released from service over a given time period, so that program formulation can develop employment opportunities that would take advantage of specific skills.

The design of a military or an economic program in a country should explicitly take into account, as *secondary* criteria of choice, the types of benefits that are primary to the other program. Although it is always difficult to obtain agreement for making changes in continuing programs, the chances of successful negotiation with the recipient countries would be increased if the necessary benefits that were sought through a proposed change were identifiable and large.

To improve coordination of economic and military plans along these lines, it might be desirable to establish several high-level coordinating positions in United States foreign missions. For example, an assistant director for economic and military planning might be established in several AID missions, say in Korea, Thailand, and Turkey; and, correspondingly, a position as assistant MAAG chief might be established, with the particular task of enhancing the economic payoffs that can be realized from military aid programs.

DEFENSE BUDGETS AND MILITARY OPERATING COSTS

The operating costs of alternative force, equipment, and infrastructure programs may be as relevant for choosing among them as the end-item, or direct MAP, costs. Sometimes introducing new equipment at a modest increase in initial costs may reduce operating and maintenance costs appreciably. For example, the operating costs per ton-mile may be considerably lower for C-118 transports than for C-47s. Newer model trucks and personnel carriers may similarly reduce operating costs. Sometimes, of course, the reverse is the case.

Under present programming procedures, operating costs often do not enter sufficiently into the choice among possible alternative military programs in a given country. Instead, they tend to be derived from a recommended military program after that program has been determined as a military requirement. From the standpoint of the efficient use of recipient countries' resources, as well as those of the United States, this is a mistaken procedure. Operating costs should be related as directly to the choice among force goals and military programs as end-item costs. In the drawing up of five-year MAP plans, operating costs should not simply be computed and identified *after* the equipment and infrastructures program has been formulated; instead, alternative forces and equipment programs should be considered for a given MAP dollar budget, and the comparison and choice among them should be based, in part, on *differences* in operating costs. The United States should be concerned with maximizing the security benefits from both MAP and local resources in a given country, not just from MAP dollars. The United States should minimize the *total* costs of buying certain security benefits, not just the MAP costs.

The general implication of this line of reasoning is that the MAAG in a particular country, with assistance from the AID mission, should, as a matter of high priority, analyze the size, composition, efficiency, and side effects of the local defense budget, and of possible alternatives to it. The aim should be to keep the defense budget from making excessive demands on available resources, and to derive benefits for the civilian economy from defense expenditures. This point, incidentally, should apply whether or not the defense budgets are ostensibly self-financed. However, one good reason for attributing some United States assistance to supporting the recipient country's defense budget in several countries is that it can provide the MAAG and the country team with an acceptable reason for investigating the local defense budget.

IMPROVING THE MIX BETWEEN
ECONOMIC AND MILITARY ASSISTANCE

In an attempt to define an appropriate balance between military and other forms of aid, one fundamental difficulty arises from the fact that the returns from military and economic aid are not readily commensurable. Hence, a judgment concerning the best aid mix requires a choice between qualitatively different end results. Another difficulty is less fundamental and more technical. Examination of alternative aid combinations is greatly facilitated if the total United States aid budget in a country has already been set. In practice, however, consideration of aid combinations may be part of the same process as consideration of the total aid budget. When *both* the mix between economic and military programs and the total budget level are variable, the problem becomes more complicated. In principle, in this case, alternative combinations of military and economic aid should be considered for *every* plausible budget total. Since limitations of time and staff preclude this, some simplification in technique is necessary.

With the aim of focusing attention directly on the gains and losses associated with alternative combinations of military and economic programs, a simplified method for dealing with the problem might have the following steps:

(1) To bracket the revelant possibilities over a five-year planning period, two differing budgets, a "high" and a "low,"[6] could be identified for each country's military aid program and for its economic aid program. In addition to the costs of military equipment, each military aid budget should include a specified amount for United States assistance to help support the recipient country's local defense budget, if necessary, as well as a general indication of the total size of the local defense budget that is associated with each military aid budget. Similarly, each economic aid budget should indicate the amount of

---

[6] In some cases a third budget, representing the current level, might well be added.

United States aid intended to provide support for the recipient country's development budget and the general size of the local development budget that should be assumed.

(2) Next, there should be an explicit statement of United States political, economic, social, and military *objectives* in each country, with separate identification of those of particular relevance to military and economic programs. These objectives, if they are to be useful in considering alternative aid mixes, should be more precise than the usual formulation of broad, loosely-stated national purposes. They should be formulated with sufficient precision so that their relationship to the amounts and kinds of aid can be identified, and that comparisons and choices among conflicting objectives can be highlighted. This will usually mean that broad aid objectives must be broken down into plausible, but more precise, military indicators (force units, combat capabilities, bases), and economic and social indicators (investment, production, employment, training and skill formation, land ownership). The military indicators can then be related to specific internal and external military threats, and the economic and social indicators related to various specific economic needs. Where specific political objectives, such as influencing a country's alliance status, supporting a particular group within the country, or extending a United States base right, enter into United States motivations, the aim should be explicitly identified together with the presumed connection between it and the magnitude or type of United States aid.

(3) In relation to the objectives set forth in Step 2, separate military and economic programs should be considered by the United States country team for the high and low budget levels. Each of these programs should represent the MAAG and AID mission's judgment of the best five-year program corresponding to each of the assumed budget levels. Some of the work involved in considering these alternative programs might be eased by providing high-speed data processing machines at the appropriate unified command to serve the few MAAGs for which this analysis might be needed.

(4) Finally, the country team should assess the political, economic, and military consequences of the four pairings of economic and mili-

tary programs. Although the high-military, low-economic, and low-military, high-economic combinations may not add to the same aid total, particular attention should be focused on these alternatives. The country team should be asked to identify its preferred choice between these combinations *and any other combinations that do not add to more than the same total budgets*, with an evaluation of the reasons for this preference. In addition, the evaluation should also answer the question of how an $X-million change above or below this preferred combination would be applied, and with what anticipated consequences. In this way, consideration of the effects of variations in the *total* aid level could be facilitated.

Clearly, decision making in Washington will have to add other considerations to those contained in the country team evaluation. For example, AID, in its role as coordinator of aid programs, must be concerned not just with varying combinations of programs *within* a country, but with varying combinations *among* countries and regions. In turn, the White House and its staff agencies must consider other public programs, and over-all federal budget claims, in making major aid budget decisions. But the foregoing steps leading to the evaluation in Step 4 can illuminate the basic issues and the country team's recommendations for resolving them.

Essentially the same method may also be of use for comparing the gains and losses that would result from accepting competing claims for funds, when there is a shortage of contingency and other funds *during* the operating year. This situation, which has often arisen, can be most satisfactorily resolved in the future by having the Department of Defense and AID (1) explicitly identify the uses to which the marginal $50 million, $100 million, or $150 million would be put if the funds were transferred from one claimant to another, and the gains expected to result from these transfers; and (2) evaluate the consequences (penalties) expected to result from dropping the marginal funds in the particular program from which funds may be transferred. On the basis of these steps, the administrator of AID could then recommend to the Secretary of State and the President the combination of these marginal uses of aid that appears preferable.

CONCLUSION

The preceding discussion focused attention on a few problems and techniques that seem to be directly relevant to improving coordination between military and economic programs. A number of important planning problems have been deliberately omitted from discussion because, though of concern to either the military or the developmental programs, they are not of particular relevance to coordination between programs. On the economic side, for example, we have not considered the problem of applying self-help and other performance criteria, as discussed in Chapter Eight, to the intercountry allocation of development aid. Similarly, no consideration has been given to the problem of whether and how long-term development planning can be emphasized without distorting the size of the public sector or diverting attention and leverage from growth-promoting fiscal, monetary, and foreign exchange policies. On the military side, problems excluded from consideration for the same reason include the techniques for determining force goals and base requirements that underlie the military assistance program, and the possibilities for, and comparative advantage of, substitution between United States and allied theater forces and facilities.

Allowing for these important omissions, some of the specific suggestions may help in improving coordination between the programs by focusing explicit attention on the alternative ways that funds can be used, and by taking directly into account the side effects of each program under consideration. However, one of the most important steps toward improved coordination is only touched on in these suggestions: namely, availability of sufficient personnel in AID, both in Washington and the field missions, who understand the military ingredients of nation building and appreciate the aims and content of the military programs; and sufficient personnel in the Department of Defense, the unified commands, and the MAAGs who understand the nonmilitary ingredients of nation building, and appreciate the aims and content of the development assistance programs. To this end, it would be desirable to have a growing exchange of personnel between AID and the Department of Defense, both in the field and in Washington, and to have personnel from each agency attend the training courses and institutes of the other. In the long run, innovations of this sort may have as much influence on improved coordination between the programs as the specific changes in planning and programming techniques discussed in this chapter.

Part
Three

EPILOGUE: RESEARCH
AND POLICY

CHAPTER TEN

Research and Policy

THE ROLE OF POLICY RESEARCH

Research can play a useful though limited role in improving public policy. Both the usefulness and the limitations are important to keep in mind.

At its best, research on policy problems can be useful in two different ways that correspond to quite different types of inquiry. One type is mainly concerned with increasing understanding, raising the level of sophistication with which policy issues are approached, opening up new lines of inquiry, and uncovering, examining, and testing the theories that implicitly underlie policy. This sort of heuristic research may cover a gamut from policy "think-pieces," to the ordering and evaluation of data, to a more rigorous formulation and testing of hypotheses using statistical and other testing methods. The aim is to sharpen and deepen perceptions and understanding on policy issues, rather than to present operationally meaningful policy or program alternatives.

The second type of research is more operational in nature, and more directly related to the formulation and evaluation of policy and program alternatives. Operational research, or "systems analysis,"[1]

---

[1] Usually, the term "operations research," or "operational research," applies to narrower problems (for example, the design, choice, or use of a particular

generally focuses on a specific policy or program: for example, the size, character, and employment of strategic offense or defense forces, or of general purpose forces; the structure of forces and supporting facilities in an alliance; military aid in a particular country or region; or the allocation of development aid among less-developed countries. Operational research views the problem under study as a system of interacting parts, and proceeds by a series of steps: first, identifying the significant interactions characterizing the system—that is, building an operational model that describes how the system works; second, specifying the policy objectives as precisely as possible; third, designing various program or policy alternatives; and finally, comparing and testing the performance of these alternatives in terms of some explicit criterion of choice that relates the alternatives to the policy objectives. In general, the testing should explicitly consider uncertainties in performance, including those that may result from the countermeasures that may be taken by an intelligent adversary. The test consists of running the alternatives through the model and choosing as the preferred alternative that which minimizes the cost of achieving a specified objective, or maximizes a particular objective for specified costs. The policy or program that meets the test becomes the recommended course of action within the confines imposed by the original operational model.

The chapters in this book illustrate both types of research, although a heuristic orientation predominates. For example, the discussions of the "value" of the third world to the United States, in Chapter One, and of political, economic and military interactions in Chapter Two, are heuristic, rather than operational. Similarly, Chapter Four on the uses and limitations of nuclear deterrence, and Chapters Five and Six, which involve statistical tests of several hypotheses concerning relationships between political, military and economic factors, are also

---

weapon system), while "systems analysis" is applied to larger and more complex systems and choices (such as the use of strategic offensive and defensive forces globally or in a particular theater of operations). For a discussion of the methods and techniques of such research, see E. S. Quade (ed.), *Analysis for Military Decisions*, Rand McNally, Chicago, 1964; and C. J. Hitch and R. N. McKean, *The Economics of Defense in A Nuclear Age*, Cambridge, Harvard University Press, 1960.

mainly concerned with clarifying issues and questioning conventional wisdom, rather than with developing improved operating programs.

On the other hand, Chapter Three, on insurgency and counterinsurgency, contains both a theoretical model for analyzing insurgency problems and several applications of this model to the task of designing counterinsurgency programs. Similarly, Chapters Seven, Eight and Nine are more operational in nature: they try to develop and apply models and methods that can help in formulating and implementing improved military and economic aid programs.

The distinction between heuristic and operational research should not be carried too far. Although heuristic work is concerned with developing new concepts and achieving a better understanding of problems, rather than with designing more effective programs, the two objectives are obviously related. The process of analyzing problems, clarifying issues, disposing of defective theories and formulating better ones, usually carries with it implications as to the kinds of programs that may be effective. If, as suggested in Chapter Three, the sources and costs of inputs that are needed by an insurgency provide a valid framework for analyzing the problem, programs concerned with countering insurgency should give major attention to just these variables. Indeed, a relevant question to ask of heuristic research on policy problems is whether (and what types of) program reorientation can be inferred from it. In the event that no program inferences can be drawn, the explanation usually is that the research in question is empty. (This is *not* the same as saying that heuristic research that does generate program implications is necessarily either competent or reliable!)

In any event, even in the best examples of heuristic research, program inferences that can be drawn may be far from providing answers to the operational question of what to include in a cost-minimizing, or effectiveness-maximizing, program. But heuristics can be helpful in suggesting where and how to look for program improvements. Thus, there is a close connection between better analysis and understanding of problems, and the formulation of better policies and programs.

In most of the chapters of this volume that deal with operational research, the focus has been on foreign aid programs. This preoccupation does not arise from a boundless faith in such programs, but, rather, from a recognition that they are among the principal instruments of United States foreign policy in the third world. Consequently, it is appropriate that research on United States policies in these areas should be concerned with foreign aid programs, and with how they can be used more effectively.

This is not to deny that there are other important instruments of United States policy in the third world. Too frequently, advocates as well as students of foreign aid lose sight of the major limitations of aid programs as policy instruments, and the relative advantages of other policy instruments in many circumstances. American military forces, for example, are among the most important of these other instruments. While it is valid to observe that the basic forces of change and modernization in the third world are political, social, and economic, the size, type, and deployments of United States military forces nevertheless remain vital instruments of policy. This fact of life is most clearly evident in crisis situations, such as that in Cuba in 1962, in the Dominican Republic in mid-1965, or in Vietnam in recent years. But even in "normal" times, the military is a vital instrument of United States policies in the less-developed countries of the world—more vital in, say, Korea and the Philippines than in India or Brazil, but generally important and pervasive. Besides military forces, there are other important instruments of policy: information programs, tariff and trade arrangements, education and cultural exchange programs, and incentives to and taxes on United States private investment. That these other important policy instruments are only occasionally referred to in this book, while the principal focus of the operational research chapters is on foreign aid programs, should not be taken as an indication of the relative importance of the various instruments.

THE LIMITATIONS OF RESEARCH

Although it is important to recognize the useful role that can be played by research, it is no less important to be aware of severe limitations on the application of research to policy problems. One type of limitation arises from a tendency of current research to be preoccupied with technique, often at the cost of substance. Something of a mystique has arisen about the techniques and equipment of modern research which occasionally suggests an almost magical capacity to effect improvements in policies and programs, as well as a presumption that the greater the use of elaborate techniques and larger computers, the better the research product. Such claims—even in less exaggerated form—are misleading and hazardous.

As already noted, the methods of systematic analysis can be useful in improving policy and program formulation. Indeed, the methodological precepts that are most useful are as simple as they are neglected: developing and comparing alternatives explicitly; identifying side effects and taking explicit account of the numerous and sometimes conflicting objectives underlying policy; allowing for uncertainties and trying to anticipate or to simulate the countermeasures of an intelligent adversary. In applying these precepts, use can often be made of computers, of linear and dynamic programming, of "gaming" and simulations, and of other advanced techniques. (Actually, in most of the relevant and influential policy studies that have been done at major research institutions in recent years, relatively simple techniques—in statistics, game theory, cost analysis, and econometrics —have tended to be more useful than complex and elaborate ones.)

But technique, whether simple or complex, is only useful when grounded in detailed knowledge about particular problems and areas —knowledge that, on many of the problems discussed in this book, is often extremely hard to acquire. Knowledge must guide the technique, not the other way around. When the procedure is reversed, the result may be a fascination with technique as a goal in itself, and a research product heavily laden with elaborate irrelevancies. The research community, as well as the consumers of its output, is, in other words, not immune to the weakness described in the fable about the king who wore no clothes. If research is technically elaborate and "up-to-date," it is sometimes accepted as good.

This type of research limitation, of course, applies to misguided and ill-conceived research—to research that is preoccupied with technical gadgetry and with impressing the audience, rather than with advancing the problem. But even research that is well-conceived and avoids an excessive preoccupation with technique confronts basic limitations in its contributions to policy. These limitations include the serious deficiencies of data, both in extent and in reliability, that apply especially to policy research on the less-developed countries. Although tremendous improvements have been and are being made in reducing these deficiences, research results must usually be severely qualified because of the imperfect character of the data on which they are based.

The limitations of research extend beyond data problems. Fundamentally, the limitations derive from the truism that the real world is vastly more complex than the modeled world that appears in all research activities. Whenever research moves into the realm of operational systems analysis, it confronts a painful choice between completeness and feasibility. If, attempting to simulate the real world, we strive for completeness, the inevitable result is a cumbersome model and a research enterprise that is infeasible to carry out. If we insist on feasibility, we get it by sacrificing completeness. Clearly, the choice must always be to sacrifice completeness, even though a continuing effort is made to extend the limits of "feasibility" by building larger research enterprises and bigger computing machines. The trick, of course, is to assure that the real-world complexities which are excluded from research models are not essentials. But the trick is always hard, and frequently impossible, to bring off. The result is that many factors that are important in policy making and to policy makers elude even sophisticated research models because it is not clear how such factors can be taken into account. These factors may include, for example, domestic political constraints in the United States, and political and psychological attitudes and reactions abroad. We have referred on several occasions to the importance of such considerations: in Chapter One, dealing with the value of the third world; in Chapters Three and Four, relating to counterinsurgency and deterrence; in Chapter Seven, concerning the evaluation of alternative military assistance programs; and in Chapter Eight, in connection with the measurement of self-help. Indeed, the utility of even the best policy research is often limited by the exclusion of some consideration that is important in the real world.

In evaluating policy research, it is a good idea to raise explicitly the question of what may have been left out that is pertinent to the formulation of policy for a particular country or on a particular problem. A researcher who can answer persuasively that nothing has been left out, or that what has been left out is not material to the choice of a preferred policy, is in an unusual and enviable position. Moreover, he is probably wrong.

Analysis of Variance for Data on Political Development in Latin America

I am indebted to Professor Fitzgibbon for making available the original survey results for all participating respondents so that the validity of the data could be tested. As a test of the meaning and informational content of the Fitzgibbon data, a standard variance test was performed according to the following procedure:

1. The separate scores of the participating respondents were grouped by countries, yielding a distribution of scores for all respondents for each of the twenty countries. This was done separately for the three surveys in 1950, 1955, and 1960, with the number of participating respondents growing from ten to twenty to forty.

2. For each of the three surveys, the variation in respondents' scores *within* the country groups was compared with the variation in the average scores *among* country groups, using the F-test.

If the information provided by the respondents is statistically meaningful, we would expect less variation in the scores estimated by all the respondents for a given country than in the average scores among the countries. The results of the F-test provide strong confirmation that the Fitzgibbon data are meaningful in this sense. For the 1950 survey (twenty countries and ten respondents) the value of F is greater than 39; for 1955 (twenty countries and twenty respondents) F is greater than 71; and for 1960 (twenty countries and forty respondents) F is 189. These F values are significant at a .005 level, adjusted for degrees of freedom. The chance of getting variance ratios as high as these is less than 1 in 200 on a random basis.

It is also of interest to note that the value of F, and the significance of F adjusted for degrees of freedom, rise as the number of respondents increased between 1950 and 1960. This indicates that the within-group variance increases less in proportion to the increase in among-group variance as expert respondents are added, which is another indication that in fact the respondents are providing something different from random judgments in their evaluation. Of course, the question of whether this "something different" should be regarded as expertise, ethnocentricity, or prejudice is not answered by these tests.

Military Outlays and
Political Change Groupings
in Latin America

TABLE B-1   *Groupings by Total Military Aid
and Political Change*

	RISE IN POLITICAL RANKING (GROUP A)	NO RISE IN POLITICAL RANKING (GROUP B)	TOTAL
Total MAP exceeds median (Group I)	(4) Peru, Venezuela, Dominican Republic, Mexico	(5) Uruguay, Chile, Ecuador, Brazil, Colombia	9
Total MAP does not exceed median (Group II)	(4) Bolivia, El Salvador, Costa Rica, Argentina	(6) Nicaragua, Honduras, Guatemala, Paraguay, Haiti, Panama	10
TOTAL	8	11	N=19

Source: Text Tables 5-1 and 5-2.

TABLE B-2   *Groupings by Per Capita Military Aid and Political Change*

	RISE IN POLITICAL RANKING (GROUP A)	NO RISE IN POLITICAL RANKING (GROUP B)	TOTAL
Per capita MAP aid exceeds median (Group III)	(3) Peru, Venezuela, Dominican Republic	(6) Uruguay, Chile, Ecuador, Brazil, Colombia, Nicaragua	9
Per capita MAP aid does not exceed median (Group IV)	(5) Mexico, Bolivia, El Salvador, Costa Rica, Argentina	(5) Honduras, Guatemala, Paraguay, Haiti, Panama	10
TOTAL	8	11	N=19

Source: Text Tables 5-1 and 5-2.

TABLE B-3   *Groupings by Average Annual Defense Outlays and Political Change*

	RISE IN POLITICAL RANKING (GROUP A)	NO RISE IN POLITICAL RANKING (GROUP B)	TOTAL
Total defense outlays exceed median (Group I)	(4) Argentina, Mexico, Peru, Venezuela	(3) Brazil, Chile, Colombia	7
Total defense outlays do not exceed median (Group II)	(2) Costa Rica, El Salvador	(5) Bolivia, Ecuador, Guatemala, Haiti, Honduras	7
TOTAL	6	8	N=14

Source: Text Tables 5-1 and 5-3.

TABLE B-4   *Groupings by Annual Per Capita Defense Outlays and Political Change*

	RISE IN POLITICAL RANKING (GROUP A)	NO RISE IN POLITICAL RANKING (GROUP B)	TOTAL
Per capita defense outlays exceed median (Group III)	(3) Argentina, Peru, Venezuela	(4) Brazil, Chile, Colombia, Ecuador	7
Per capita defense outlays do not exceed median (Group IV)	(3) Costa Rica, El Salvador, Mexico	(4) Bolivia, Guatemala, Haiti, Honduras	7
TOTAL	6	8	N=14

Source: Text Tables 5-1 and 5-3.

Economic-Indicators and Political Change Groupings in Latin America

TABLE C-1 *Groupings by Per Capita GNP and Political Change*

	RISE IN POLITICAL RANKING	NO RISE IN POLITICAL RANKING	TOTAL
Average annual per capita GNP exceeds median	(5) Argentina, Costa Rica, Dominican Republic, Mexico, Venezuela	(4) Chile, Colombia, Nicaragua, Panama	9
Average annual per capita GNP does not exceed median	(3) Bolivia, El Salvador, Peru	(6) Brazil, Ecuador, Guatemala, Haiti, Honduras, Paraguay	9
TOTAL	8	10	N=18

Source: Text Tables 5-1 and 6-1.

TABLE C-2   *Groupings by Gross Capital Formation-to-GNP (Per Cent) and Political Change*

	RISE IN POLITICAL RANKING	NO RISE IN POLITICAL RANKING	TOTAL
Average annual gross investment/GNP exceeds median	(5) Argentina, Costa Rica, Dominican Republic, Peru, Venezuela	(2) Brazil, Colombia	7
Average annual gross investment/GNP does not exceed median	(2) Bolivia, Mexico	(6) Chile, Ecuador, Guatemala, Haiti, Honduras, Panama	8
	7	8	N=15

Source: Text Tables 5-1 and 6-1.

TABLE C-3   *Groupings by Capital Formation Per Capita and Political Change*

	RISE IN POLITICAL RANKING	NO RISE IN POLITICAL RANKING	TOTAL
Per capita gross investment exceeds median	(5) Argentina, Costa Rica, Mexico, Peru, Venezuela	(2) Chile, Panama	7
Per capita gross investment does not exceed median	(2) Bolivia, Dominican Republic	(6) Brazil, Colombia, Ecuador, Guatemala, Haiti, Honduras	8
TOTAL	7	8	N=15

Source: Text Tables 5-1 and 6-1.

Selected Bibliography

Almond, G. A., and J. S. Coleman (eds.), *The Politics of the Developing Areas*, Princeton, Princeton University Press, 1960.

Banfield, Edward C., *American Foreign Aid Doctrines*, Washington, D. C., American Enterprise Institute for Public Policy Research, 1963.

Becker, G. S., "Underinvestment in College Education," *American Economic Review Proceedings*, Vol. 50, No. 2, May 1960, pp. 346–354.

Black, Eugene R., *The Diplomacy of Economic Development*, Cambridge, Massachusetts, Harvard University Press, 1960.

Blanksten, George, "Fidel Castro and Latin America," in Morton A. Kaplan (ed.), *The Revolution in World Politics*, New York, John Wiley & Sons, 1962.

Brinton, Crane, *The Anatomy of Revolution*, New York, Vintage Books (rev. 1962).

Chenery, H. B., "Patterns of Industrial Growth," *American Economic Review*, Vol. 50, No. 4, September 1960, pp. 624–654.

Clark, Paul G., *Indicators of Self-Help*, Washington, D. C., Agency for International Development, 1962.

Coleman, James S., "The Political Systems of the Developing Areas," in G. A. Almond and J. S. Coleman (eds.), *The Politics of the Developing Areas*, Princeton, Princeton University Press, 1960.

Cross, James E., *Conflict in the Shadows: The Nature and Politics of Guerrilla War*, New York, Doubleday and Co., Inc., 1963.

Dean, Vera Micheles, "Southeast Asia and Japan," in James Roosevelt (ed.), *The Liberal Papers*, New York, Doubleday and Co., Inc., 1962.

Export-Import Bank, *Semiannual and Annual Reports, 1950–1960*, Washington, D. C., 1950-1961.

Fall, Bernard, *Street Without Joy*, Harrisburg, The Stackpole Co., 1963.

Finer, S. E., *The Man on Horseback: The Role of the Military in Politics*, New York, Frederick A. Praeger, Inc., 1962.

Fitzgibbon, Russell H., "How Democratic Is Latin America?" *Inter-American Economic Affairs*, Vol. 9, No. 4, Spring 1956, pp. 65–77.

————, "Measurement of Latin American Political Phenomena: A Statistical Experiment," *American Political Science Review*, Vol. 45, No. 2, June 1951, pp. 517–523.

————, "A Statistical Evaluation of Latin American Democracy," *Western Political Quarterly*, Vol. 9, No. 3, September 1956, pp. 607–619.

Friedman, Milton, "Foreign Economic Aid: Means and Objectives," *The Yale Review*, Vol. 47, No. 4, Summer 1958, pp. 500–516.

Furniss, Edgar S., Jr., *Some Perspectives on American Military Assistance*, Princeton, Center for International Studies, 1957.

Galula, David, *Counter-Insurgency Warfare: Theory and Practice*, New York, Frederick A. Praeger, Inc., 1964.

Geiger, Theodore, and L. Solomon (eds.), *Motivations and Methods in Development and Foreign Aid*, Washington, D. C., Society for International Development, 1964.

Ginsburg, Norton, *Atlas of Economic Development*, Chicago, University of Chicago Press, 1961.

Greene, T. N. (ed.), *The Guerrilla—and How to Fight Him*, New York, Frederick A. Praeger, Inc., 1962.

Hagen, Everett E., "A Framework for Analyzing Economic and Political Change," in Asher, Hagen, *et al.*, *Development of the Emerging Countries*, Washington, D. C., The Brookings Institution, 1962.

Halperin, Morton H., "Chinese Nuclear Strategy: The Early Post-Detonation Period," *Adelphi Papers Number 18*, London, Institute of Strategic Studies, 1965.

Higgins, Benjamin, *Economic Development*, New York, W. W. Norton, 1959.

Hirschman, Albert O., *Journeys Toward Progress*, New York, Twentieth Century Fund, 1963.

————, *The Strategy of Economic Development*, New Haven, Yale University Press, 1958.

Hoffer, Eric, *The True Believer*, New York, Harper & Bros., 1952.

Houthakker, H., "An International Comparison of Personal Savings," *Bulletin of the International Statistical Association*, Vol. 38, Part 2, 1961, pp. 55–69.

————, "On Some Determinants of Savings in Developed and Underdeveloped Countries" (Memorandum No. 20, mimeographed), Stanford, Stanford Research Center in Economic Growth, July 1962.

India, Government of, *Report of the Taxation Enquiry Commission, 1953–1954*, New Delhi, 1955.

India, Government of, Planning Commission, *Third Five-Year Plan—A Draft Outline*, New Delhi, 1960.

International Monetary Fund, *International Financial Statistics,* various monthly issues, 1957–1962.

Johnson, John J. (ed.), *The Role of the Military in Underdeveloped Countries,* Princeton, Princeton University Press, 1962.

Jordan, Amos A., Jr., *Foreign Aid and the Defense of Southeast Asia,* New York, Frederick A. Praeger, Inc., 1962.

Kahn, Herman, *On Escalation: Scenarios and Metaphors,* New York, Frederick A. Praeger, Inc., 1965.

Kuznets, Simon, "Quantitative Aspects of the Economic Growth of Nations; V: Capital Formation Proportions: International Comparisons for Recent Years," *Economic Development and Cultural Change,* Vol. 8, No. 4, Part 2, July 1960, pp. 1–96.

Lieuwen, Edwin, *Arms and Politics in Latin America,* New York, published for the Council on Foreign Relations by Frederick A. Praeger, Inc., 1960.

Lipset, Seymour, "Some Social Requisites of Democracy: Economic Development and Political Legitimacy," *American Political Science Review,* Vol. 53, No. 1, March 1959, pp. 69–105.

Lockwood, William W., *The Economic Development of Japan,* Princeton, Princeton University Press, 1954.

Malenbaum, Wilfred, *Prospects for Indian Development,* Glencoe, Illinois, The Free Press, 1962.

Mason, Edward S., *Economic Planning in Underdeveloped Areas: Government and Business,* New York, Fordham University Press, 1958.

———, *Foreign Aid and Foreign Policy,* New York, Harper and Row, 1964.

Matthews, H. L., "When Generals Take Over in Latin America," *The New York Times Magazine,* September 9, 1962, pp. 56 ff.

McClelland, David, *The Achieving Society,* Princeton, D. Van Nostrand Company, Inc., 1961.

Meisler, Stanley, "Small Arms-Race," *The Nation,* Vol. 190, No. 16, April 16, 1960, pp. 332–335.

Melman, Seymour, *The Peace Race,* New York, George Braziller, 1961.

Millikan, Max F., and W. W. Rostow, *A Proposal: Key to an Effective Foreign Policy,* New York, Harper & Bros., 1957.

National Council of Applied Economic Research, *Urban Income and Saving,* New Delhi, published for the National Council of Applied Economic Research by Hoe & Co., 1962.

Olson, Mancur, Jr., "Rapid Growth as a Destabilizing Force," *Journal of Economic History,* Vol. 23, No. 4, December 1963.

Paauw, Douglas S., *Financing Economic Development: The Indonesian Case,* Glencoe, Illinois, The Free Press, 1960.

Pauker, Guy J., "Southeast Asia as a Problem Area in the Next Decade," *World Politics*, Vol. 11, No. 3, April 1959, pp. 325–345.

Romulo, Carlos P., and Marvin M. Gray, *The Magsaysay Story*, Toronto, Longmans, 1956.

Rosen, George, *Democracy and Economic Change in India*, Berkeley and Los Angeles, University of California Press, 1966.

Schlesinger, James R., *The Political Economy of National Security*, New York, Frederick A. Praeger, Inc., 1960.

Shils, Edward, *Political Development in the New States*, The Hague, Mouton & Co., 1962.

Tannenbaum, Frank, "Considerations for the Latin American Policy," in James Roosevelt (ed.), *The Liberal Papers*, New York, Doubleday and Co., Inc., 1962.

Tocqueville, Alexis de, *The Old Regime and the French Revolution*, New York, Doubleday and Co., Inc., 1955.

United Nations Economic Commission for Asia and the Far East, *Economic Survey of Asia and the Far East*, New York, United Nations, 1960–1965.

United Nations Statistical Office, *Demographic Yearbooks*, 1959–1963, New York, United Nations, 1960–1964.

———, *Statistical Yearbook*, Volumes for 1954 through 1964, New York, United Nations, 1955–1965.

———,*Yearbooks of International Trade Statistics*, 1960–1963, New York, United Nations, 1962–1965.

———, *Yearbooks of National Accounts Statistics*, 1957–1964, New York, United Nations, 1958–1965.

United States, The President's Committee to Study the Military Assistance Program (The Draper Committee), *Composite Report*, Vols. I and II, Washington, D. C., 1959.

United States Agency for International Development, *Regional Data Books for Latin America, Near East and South Asia, and Far East* (loose-leaf folders), 1962–1965.

———, Program Coordinating Staff, *Principles of Foreign Economic Assistance*, Washington, D. C., 1963.

United States Department of Defense, Director of Military Assistance, *Military Assistance Programs—Programs and Deliveries, FY 1950–1961*, Washington, D. C., 1961.

United States International Cooperation Administration, *Operations Reports*, Washington, D. C., 1961–1965.

United States Senate, *Foreign Assistance Acts of 1962–1965*, Hearings, Committee on Foreign Relations, 87th Congress, Second Session, Washington, D. C., 1962–1965.

————, *Foreign Assistance Acts of 1962–1965*, Hearings, Committee on Foreign Relations, 88th Congress, First Session, Washington, D. C., 1962–1965.

————, *International Development and Security*, Hearings, Committee on Foreign Relations, 87th Congress, First Session, Washington, D. C., 1961.

————, *Mutual Security Act of 1957*, Hearings, Committee on Foreign Relations, 85th Congress, First Session, Washington, D. C., 1957.

————, *Vietnam and Southeast Asia*, Report, Committee on Foreign Relations, 88th Congress, First Session, Washington, D. C., 1963.

Wald, Haskell P., and Joseph N. Froomkin, *Agricultural Taxation and Economic Development*, Cambridge, Massachusetts, Harvard University Press, 1954.

Weiner, M. G., *War Gaming Methodology*, Santa Monica, The RAND Corporation, RM–2413, July 1959.

Weisbrod, B. A., "The Valuation of Human Capital," *Journal of Political Economy*, Vol. 69, No. 5, October 1961, pp. 425–436.

Wolf, Charles, Jr., *Foreign Aid: Theory and Practice in Southern Asia*, Princeton, Princeton University Press, 1960.

Index